WEST YORKSHIRE
WITHIN LIVING MEMORY

—◆—

WEST YORKSHIRE

WITHIN LIVING MEMORY

—◆—

Compiled by the West Yorkshire Federation
of Women's Institutes from contributions sent by
Institutes in the County

Published jointly by
Countryside Books, Newbury
and the WYFWI, Leeds

First published 1996
© West Yorkshire Federation of Women's Institutes 1996

COUNTRYSIDE BOOKS
3 Catherine Road
Newbury, Berkshire

ISBN 1 85306 399 1

Front cover photograph supplied by Irene Broadfield, Woodkirk Valley WI
Back cover photograph supplied by Betty Leach, Cottingley & District WI

Produced through MRM Associates Ltd., Reading
Printed by Woolnough Bookbinding Ltd, Irthlingborough

CONTENTS

▣ TOWN & COUNTRY LIFE   *page 9*
Some towns and villages remembered – church and chapel –
getting about.

▣ HOUSE & HOME   *page 41*
The way we lived then – water and washday –
food and shopping – street traders – from the cradle to the
grave.

▣ CHILDHOOD & SCHOOLDAYS   *page 81*
Childhood days – games and treats – schooldays: the best years
of our lives?

▣ THE WORLD OF WORK   *page 115*
On the land – mining memories – in the mills – other ways we
made a living.

▣ WAR & PEACE   *page 153*
The Great War 1914–1918 – the Second World War 1939–1945 – a
child's war – the evacuees – doing our bit.

▣ HIGHDAYS & HOLIDAYS   *page 195*
Making our own entertainment – Royal days – all through the
year.

The West Riding
of Yorkshire
(until All Fools' Day, 1974)

The Dales

·Sedbergh

SHEEP
CATTLE
MILK
CEREALS
Ripon

CATTLE
SHEEP

SHEEP

Shipton

Harrogate

York

Keighley

MARKET
GARDENING

Leeds

CLOTHING
PIGS
COAL

Bradford

COAL

CEREALS

Halifax

WOOLLENS

Wakefield

N

WOOLLENS
CHEMICALS
Huddersfield

(not to scale)

West Yorkshire boundary
since 1974   — — — — —

COAL

CEREALS

Sheffield
·
IRON AND STEEL

WEST YORKSHIRE

FOREWORD

Since the turn of the century there have been so many changes to our way of life that would have been hard to imagine back in 1900. The changes have taken place in the home and workplace both urban and rural. West Yorkshire is well known for its hills, dales, moors, mills and mines, providing a wealth of different lifestyles that show the determination and perseverance that have taken place to overcome the many difficulties in changing fortunes.

Until 1973 the area was known as the West Riding but with local government and boundary changes we became known as West Yorkshire.

We hope that this book will give readers nostalgic memories and an insight into the past, through the memories of all aspects of life in West Yorkshire, both serious and trivial.

Marion Walker
County Chairman

ACKNOWLEDGEMENTS

West Yorkshire Federation of Women's Institutes would like to thank all W.I. members, family and friends who contributed material for this book. Unfortunately, we have not been able to include extracts from every submission as this would have caused some duplication of content but all contributions were of value in compiling the book.

We would like to thank Barbara Gardner and Rosemary Walton for co-ordinating, typing many manuscripts and transcribing tapes; Brian Husband for the county map and the Chapter illustrations; Ken Gardner for the drawing of the County badge; Pip Challenger for additional line drawings; Horsforth Village Museum for help with photographs, and Janet Ripley for introducing the idea to members.

TOWN & COUNTRY LIFE

Some Towns and Villages Remembered

Life has changed so much over the past few decades that it is sometimes hard to remember that as children we lived in a vastly different world. Here are just a few snapshot memories – including promming in Pudsey, the snows of 1947, and family life in Castleford.

▣ Leeds in the 1930s ▣

'One of my early memories is of looking across the famous Briggate in Leeds on winter afternoons in the mid 1930s and seeing the wonderful neon lights on the taller buildings, especially the large Schweppes and Bovril ones as their colours fanned out.

My parents ran a dressmaking business two floors up over a tobacconist's shop; Father was manager, cutter-out and presser, and made a work of art out of wrapping finished garments in tissue paper and brown carrier bags. Mother and her sister did the sewing and fitting, and "pinning up". My brother and I helped by picking up all the loose pins from the lino with the giant magnet.

We were not latch-key kids – somehow one parent or auntie always managed to be home for us, but in the school holidays, and on Saturdays (the five-day week was yet to be invented!) we would go into town with them on the tram, and hang around in the workroom, hampering the other sewing ladies no doubt.

Backstairs in that building was very dark and dingy, with prehistoric lavatories, dark brown lincrusta on the walls, and hardly any lights on the stairs – conditions which would never be allowed nowadays, but pretty general, I think, in those days.

EAGLE INN (SILENT INN) AND COLNE ROAD, STANBURY.

The road from Stanbury leading over the moors to Colne and Lancashire – a timeless scene. The mill in the valley bottom is now a great tourist attraction as a mill shop – the original Ponden Mill.

Almost opposite our windows was the famous old Empire Theatre. (A lifetime later, it seemed, I was to spend many happy hours there enjoying variety shows.) Quite a number of our customers were showgirls from the theatre, especially when Mother branched out for a while into ready-made summer dresses. This seemed to come about when printed cotton fabrics became easier to produce, and could be had in vast varieties for 1s 11½d and 2s 11½d per yard, being sold by Hitchen's store, where we also bought most of our haberdashery, Matthias Robinson's store, Schofield's round the corner, and many more famous names from those days.

This was also the time when the builders were adding two extra floors at the top of Lewis's store, and I remember seeing that amazing new white Queen's Hotel grow in City Square, where I believe it replaced an older one.

With the current nostalgia for old photographs of tram-filled city streets, I am back there again gazing from those second-floor windows watching the ever-changing crowds thronging old Briggate. But my favourite memory of those pre-war days is of

Saturday lunch-time sitting on a high stool around the huge cutting-out table, eating soft white teacakes from Lyons' corner shop, spread with fish-paste which came weighed out in a "screw" of greaseproof paper!'

▣ PROMMING AT PUDSEY ▣

'In the year 1944 my father was curator of Pudsey Town Hall; he later became Mace Bearer. Each Saturday and Sunday evening I went with him to stoke up the boiler in the Town Hall. I can smell the coke now as he shovelled it into the boiler with a massive shovel. After that he used to say, "Shall we join in the promming?", which went from way down Lowtown to Chapeltown. In those far away days there were few cars or buses so the "Prommers" stretched right across the road and onto the pavements at each side of the road. It was packed solid with people just walking up and down this road, time and time again – just talking and laughing. There was never any trouble.

In the Maypole shop doorway a man with a wicker laundry basket used to sell celery hearts; he was there every weekend.'

▣ KIRKBURTON CHILDHOOD ▣

'When I was a child I lived in a village called Kirkburton. I lived in a road just below the station with a high wall and banking full of trees and above that was what we always referred to as the station gates. At the end outside the gates were brick stables which housed the big cart horses, used to pull the wagons that delivered the goods that came up on the train.

Going back to the time when I was about eight years old and the 1926 coal strike was on and they were out-cropping, some friends of mine and I used to go and pick small coal off the out-crop. We could fill a small cart for 1d; the carts were made out of orange boxes with old pram wheels. My friend's dad made one for me. We had to go down what we called Spider Alley, two long walls with a stile at each end, and we had to take turns to lift the carts over the stiles.

The train that ran between Kirkburton and Huddersfield was

Lidget Hill, Oakworth in 1930 and (below) Oakworth in the snow in 1955.

called Burton Dick. Each spring we went to town on the train and bought my Whitsuntide clothes, then we would go again for winter things. That, of course, was before my dad died, after that money was short.

When I was growing up we had what we called pedlars who came to the door with trays and boxes of buttons, elastic, tape etc. Mum always tried to spend a few coppers with them; some of them must have walked miles for coppers. We used to have one old man with a long white beard and if Mum gave him sixpence he would put it between his teeth and it trembled. I was fascinated, thinking it was going to go down but it never did.

We also had an old lady, a real gypsy who came round; she said she had never slept in a house. Mum used to give her a stool and she sat in the front porch, then Mum made her a pint of tea after which she sat and smoked her little clay pipe. No one ever went short of a cup of tea – workmen and men working on the road were always sure of a cup of tea, without charge.

The street that I lived in was very steep and cobbled and the carts carrying coal, pulled by two horses, went up and down. I have seen the horses slip and go down and not be able to get up because of the weight in the cart, and every man who was at home would come out when the horses were down. They would undo the harnesses, then shout "Stand back", because as soon as the weight was taken off the horses they would jump up and the men would hold the coal cart. In those days people helped each other without expecting any return.

Talking about coal, my mother had a brother who was a policeman in Featherstone and she used to take me to see him. On the way we would see children with bare feet, and I would say why haven't they got shoes and socks on? I was too young to realize what the strike had done to people. I have seen the children sliding down the slag heap on bits of cardboard with no seat in their trousers. It was beyond my understanding at that age.

When I got to be 14 years old I left school. I went to work in the mill just behind our house. I can remember running down the mill lane on a dark morning and woe betide you if you were a minute late. The foreman stood in the yard and if you were late he made you go home till breakfast time and so you lost money on your wage. Eleven shillings and elevenpence a week, and Mum gave me one shilling back for myself.

When I was growing up my cousin from next door worked as a porter on the railway. Later he became a goods man, and every year he would get up a trip by train to see Blackpool Illuminations. In those days the people who worked there used to take quite a pride in their stations and they would have gardens all along the platform and behind the buffers, picking out the name of the station with plants and pebbles. As I remember, my cousin won some prizes for this.

Down the road from where I lived was an old pub called the Railway Junction and outside in the open sheds I have been taken to see the pot market all lit up with the big hanging flares. The pub has now been modernized and renamed.'

▩ A CASTLEFORD FAMILY ▩

'Soon after my grandparents, William and Annie Fox, were married, they moved into a two bedroomed house in Houghton Street. They lived near the bottom of the row of about 20 homes. William's parents and brothers lived in two houses further up the row, other relatives lived nearby. These homes were probably built for the families of miners, as the colliery was less than 440 yards away. All the houses had odd numbers, the owners must have intended to build opposite, but this row never materialised, instead the residents of Houghton Street had a beautiful view of the Castleford branch railway line, high on its embankment.

At the top of the street was a shop. The shopkeeper made up little packets of one cigarette and a match which the miners smoked on the way down to the mine. They were not allowed to take combustibles down the mine, for safety.

My mother still remembers her father describing some of the conditions he experienced down the mine: "He used to tie billy-bands round his legs to stop the rats running up inside his trousers. The miners could see the rats' eyes shining at them whilst working down the mine. They used to build a pyramid with stones to prevent the rats getting at the food inside the snap tins."

15

COAT OF ARMS

of the

COUNTY COUNCIL OF THE

WEST RIDING

OF YORKSHIRE

The coat of arms for the old West Riding of Yorkshire.

When Grandad came home from work, the tin bath was brought in from its hook in the yard by the back door, for him to bathe in front of the fire. The children were bathed there also, but Mum never saw her mum get bathed. She wondered if she got bathed after they were all in bed.

Some miners were conscripted into the army in 1916. I do not think Grandad would have gone from choice, as he left behind a pregnant wife with three children under five years of age. His return from the war made a strong impression on his children as both my mother and uncle gave the same descriptions: "When Dad came home from the war, he used to jump over the wall opposite our house. He must have jumped out of the train as it slowed down for Castleford station. He had his kitbag, and I can still see him sitting outside the door unwinding those khaki strips around his legs, puttees I think they were called. Before he went to war he used to play with us, laugh and tell us jokes. When he came back he just sat by the fire not talking to us."

After the war he returned to the mines, working underground as a byworker. I have been told that a byworker was sent to do any job in the mine, wherever he was needed. I do not know how long he was able to work, but he died in October 1920, 36 years old.

After becoming a widow, my grandmother married James Digby. My mother puzzled over how they met: "I don't know how they met, because he was living with his sister, Rose on Duke Street. Maybe it was at the club on Wheldon Lane. Mum used to get dressed up and go there some nights, he was on the committee there. The committee members used to get a free pint, but he was tee-total, maybe they gave him a cigar instead.

"He was a gentle, kind man, every Sunday he would put out little heaps of sweets for us. Grace and I used to get extra, probably because we did more work. We didn't have toys, but there was one clockwork toy which he kept in the cupboard, too high for us to reach, if we had we would have broken it fighting over it. We all used to stand and watch him wind it up and let it go round and round."

Their new father was also a miner, a coal hewer, but he also had an allotment where he grew prize-winning vegetables and he often went out shooting rabbits for the family to eat; they had good meals. My grandmother used to make pies and leave them on the doorstep to cool. As Mum remarked, "They can't have had many dogs around at that time."

Mum told me of many incidents which happened during her childhood: "Mum used to make our Sunday dresses. One neighbour was admiring my dress when Mum lifted up my skirt and said, 'Not only have I made the dress, but the knickers too!' I was so embarrassed. We had a Sunday school treat one day – a sail in a coal barge, which had been cleaned out for the occasion, unfortunately my dress was dirty in no time.

"I used to go to Sunday school in a church which seemed to be built of wood. One morning I had stopped in a field to pick some blue flowers to take to church. I was late but the vicar would not let me go in without a hat. He tied a hanky in four corners and put it on my head. It was enough to put anyone off church for life.

"My Gran used to buy children's comics every week, but would not let them out of her house. That was one way of making sure her grandchildren visited her every week. She wore a black lace cap all the time, with black beads hanging round it. I used to rush home from school to blacklead her grate as well as ours and my aunty's.

"The earth closets were in the backyards; my aunty's and gran's were next to each other, and ours was a bit further down the street. They had three holes in them, one a little hole. I don't know who would want to sit in together. I used to clean all three of them. The cart to collect the soil from the closets came around early in the morning, while we were in bed. After they finished they scattered white powder around. I loved looking out of the bedroom window at the glittering lights on the carts."

More children followed, Gran had nine altogether, with seven surviving to adulthood. My mother, being the second eldest, was often sent to stay with relatives nearby, as accommodation and privacy would be limited in a two bedroomed terraced house. Usually, she stayed with Aunt Rose, on Duke Street.

"Aunt Rose used to bake apple pies to sell, she put them in the house window. It was an ordinary window, but she had it built up with wooden stands, sloping so all the pies could be seen on display. When people saw the pies go in they would queue at the door, but she didn't let them in until she was ready.

"I had to go up for the apples when they were going off a bit, she got them cheap for baking. She once sent me for some trotters. Well, I had never even heard of that word – 'trotter' – I was saying it to myself all the way up Wheldon Lane to the butcher's, and there was a right queue, they were all talking and they all wanted something different. When it became my turn, 'trotter' had completely gone. I had to go all the way back to find out what the name was.

"Aunt Rose made brawn pies, small ones, just about the right size for the men's snap tins. She made lots of other things to sell like ginger pop, using yeast and what was left of the old ginger. I helped her make ice cream; I used to turn the handle of the churn, which had pieces of ice packed round it to keep it cool. She made jelly, I wonder if she used the trotters for that."

Mum's uncle, James had a milk round and land near the Wheldon Road Rugby Club for his cows. He and Aunt Sophia also sold milk from home. Customers who knocked on the door were never allowed in, not even relatives. He had a disabled sister who sat in a dark corner of the room, in charge of the money.

Mum recalls her grandfather as being a plump little "fella". Her brother, John, has vivid memories of his death in 1926: "I can remember when Grandad died, it was during the miners' strike. He was up in the muck heaps, scrabbling for bits of coal for his family when he collapsed. I wasn't sure he was dead, but when I got home I found the toilet door gone. They had taken it to bring him home, and they laid him out on it. They always did that in those days, when you saw the toilet door missing you knew that somebody was dead."

John also recalls an incident at Hickson's Chemical Works in the 1930s: "When Hickson's blew up at five to twelve one Friday, girders fell on Uncle Jim's cowshed, as well as damaging houses nearby. On Sunday people came from all over to look at the damage. Local lads would be around. "Show you girders, sir," we would say to get a few coppers. People would show stuff from their houses which had been damaged, stuff like picture frames, which had dirt in the cracks from long before this event."

My grandmother became ill after the birth of her ninth child and Mother had to leave school early to become the housekeeper: "If we needed anything for the housekeeping, we would take it from Dad's coat pocket because he was working down the mine. Grace worked at Bellamy's sweet factory, which was on the way into town. She would stick lumps of rock into her apron for the others to eat when she got home.

"I remember the day my mum died I was sitting on the floor by the fire, with Grace, reading. Mum was resting on the sofa, she was expecting another baby. When I started to make a noise, Grace went, 'Sssh, be quiet, Mum needs the rest.' Later, when we walked over to see how she was, she had died. When my dad came home, he went berserk, he must have loved her a lot. He had two guns on the wall, he took one down and tried to kill himself. The neighbours rushed in and held him down and managed to stop him." She was only 37 years old when she died, two days before her eldest daughter's 16th birthday.'

▨ THE BIG SNOW OF 1947 ▨

'The year 1947 stands out as a memorable year when I was aged 22. The snow lasted for six weeks during which time I helped my father to reach stranded homes with a daily supply of milk. My father had purchased an ex-army vehicle for his deliveries, an opportune time, in fact, as we lived in quite a rural area adjoining woodland at Cragg Wood, Rawdon. Our neighbours were housebound each day until my father opened up the road, the snow was six or seven feet deep in parts and only by constant usage were footpaths kept cleared.

I can well remember walking down an area known as Low Green, seeing the top of a lamp post at knee level. A local farmer literally slid down this footpath on his bottom for the distance of half a mile to reach his livestock each day. Sadly, this exercise proved too much for him and he died before the thaw came at the end of March.

I remember the floods that followed and on outings to the local dales seeing cows and sheep lying dead in the fields. We were rewarded by having a beautiful summer, long weeks of hot sunny days.'

'In the big snow of 1947 I lived at the top of Norwood Edge. All the roads thereabouts were filled with snow and we had to walk on the wall tops for six weeks. The German prisoners of war were employed to dig the main road out but they had no sooner got it done than the wind got up and blew it full again. The postman walked from the bottom of the hill, a distance of one and a half miles about once a week and left all the mail with us for the surrounding farms. The butcher from Otley also walked up with a big basket of meat. Luckily it kept well in the freezing temperatures as we had no fridge or freezer in those days. My mother and I walked to Otley and back occasionally and carried back any groceries that we needed, but only after the roads had been cleared of snow. Luckily we had plenty of eggs, milk, butter and bacon on the farm and always bought our flour by the sack and our coal by the ton.'

▓ I REMEMBER… ▓

'I remember the lamplighter with his pole turning the gas lamps on at night and off in the morning. The milkman with his horse and float coming to the door with his churn and measuring the milk with a ladle. The wheelwright cooling newly made wheels and the steam rising from the pond. The horses pulling barges along the canal. The malt kiln, and if the smell was strong it was a sign of rain. The coalman with his horse and cart, lifting the bags and tipping the coal down into the cellar.'

'I remember when the pawnbroker lived on Carlton Street, Cutsyke and was the only source of cash so you borrowed on his terms. If you needed money at the beginning of the week goods were handed over and when the housekeeping purse was replenished some or all of the items would be redeemed and for every pound borrowed an extra half-crown would be needed to retrieve the possessions. Goods would be left at the shop amassing debt, until after three months the shopkeeper could dispose of them for whatever they would fetch. My Mum did not believe in pawning but if she ran short of money for food she would buy two pennyworth of suet from the butcher and make a large boiled pudding with some dried fruit. This was accompanied by a big jug of custard made from "old" milk (skimmed) which could be bought for tuppence a jug.'

'My father bought the end house on Church Lane (now Church Road), Horsforth in about 1924. He was told at the time that he would lose part of his garden to the new road, and this did eventually happen – but not until the 1960s. When we lived there, it was an unmade lane and as irregular as a river bed. It was surrounded by green fields used for haymaking; we played in the haycocks, much to the annoyance of "the fat farmer". When my father came home from work, I used to enjoy riding up Church Lane on the running board of his car.

People didn't waste time on the telephone in those days. My father would ring his secretary at the mill to find out if there were any outstanding matters. He would ask, "Owt?", she would reply, "Nowt!" and that was the end of the conversation.'

❖ EAST KESWICK IN 1965 ❖

'In 1965 the following description of the village was written.

To celebrate the Golden Jubilee of the WI, East Keswick WI members planted daffodil bulbs on a high bank and roadside verges in the village. At the Duke of Wellington hotel the Bramham Moor Hunt meets. East Keswick primary school was recently enlarged by the addition of a prefabricated wing and was then able to accommodate about 70 pupils. The over-elevens travel by bus either to Tadcaster grammar school or Wetherby secondary modern school. Opposite the primary school stood the village hall – a temporary structure built after the Second World War and used for most of the village functions. In School Lane, the old flour mill has been converted into workshops and a showroom for a carpet and curtain cleaning firm. In the main street there is a very modern and well equipped butcher's shop run by the same family for many years and opposite, the post office with a mail sorting office and four full time postmen, who deliver mail to the adjoining villages and outlying districts. There are two collections a day and two deliveries. From the butcher's shop the road runs through a slight cutting and it was the soil from this cutting which buried the old Quaker burial ground.

Before reaching the Laurence Memorial Chapel there are three houses, one of which was the original butcher's shop and slaughterhouse and now a carefully modernised residence. The wooden cobbler's shop is on the corner where the entrance to The Close sweeps round into Stocks Hill, but the stocks have gone. Stocks Hill is still the official name but the small village square is often referred to as "City Square". There is a high railed footpath on the right of the road adding character and charm to the village.

On the right corner of Moor Lane, known locally as "West End", stands the Old Parsonage and a smallholding opposite. There is another grocer's shop which has been altered to resemble an old-fashioned bow-windowed shop. Still in West End and beyond the entrance to West Drive is the village church of St Mary Magdalene and opposite is the old school now used as the Men's Institute and to the west of the church is the village tennis club. There are no resident clergy in the village – the church is served by the vicar of Harewood and lay readers and the chapel by the circuit minister and local preachers. The two congregations occasionally meet for a joint service. The small community of Moorside includes a market garden, farm and a few cottages. The main part of East Keswick also has a joiner's shop, another painter and decorator, a grocer's shop and a ladies' hairdresser. On the way to Harewood are two council estates and two or three larger houses, one, The Mount was originally a girls' boarding school.

A row of lime trees was planted on the cricket ground side of the road in memory of the dead of the First World War and the WI planted crocus round these trees for the WI Golden Jubilee. The lime trees planted down the hill were to commemorate the Coronation (the Princess Royal and her two sons planted three of these) and round the small triangular Garden of Rest (halfway down the hill) are five more lime trees planted in memory of the dead of the Second World War.

The Harewood doctor holds a surgery in the village, thrice weekly although many residents are patients of the doctors at Collingham and Wetherby. The Harewood district nurse is on call and there is a child welfare clinic on alternative Mondays in the chapel schoolroom. Babies are weighed and examined by the doctor who also gives them their various inoculations; at present these are three injections of the triple vaccine against diphtheria, whooping cough and tetanus (given at two, three and four months of age), the polio oral vaccine (at about six, seven and eight months of age) and the smallpox vaccination (after the first birthday). Older children sometimes attend for booster doses of the vaccines. Baby food is sold at the Welfare price (a 4s packet of baby milk from the shop is 3s 1d at the clinic) as is rose hip syrup, Marmite etc. A very welcome cup of tea is served for 3d to the mothers by ladies from the chapel who take turns in attending.'

CHURCH AND CHAPEL

Sundays were special, when attendance at church or chapel – and Sunday school for children – was part of the weekly routine. Sunday school treats were often a highlight of the year for children who had few other outings, and the church was a social centre for the community.

▨ BEST CLOTHES FOR CHAPEL ▨
'We never wore our best, Whitsuntide, clothes on Monday. They were just for Sunday – change when you got home from Sunday school and chapel in the morning, change back after dinner for Sunday school in the afternoon and again when you got home.'

◼ BUT WOMEN WERE ALLOWED TO COOK! ◼

'You were not allowed to work even if you were willing, although women were allowed to cook. Children were not allowed to play out on Sundays – or even play in – and no one was allowed to use scissors on the Sabbath. It was easier to keep the Sabbath in the winter when the days were short and cold. The arrival of the gas lamp at the end of the street extended the hours one could play outside but on Sundays the man didn't come to light the lamp.

Our best rug was always brought down on Sundays and our evenings would usually be spent working on the next. Sunday clothes were worn and enforced inactivity helped to ensure that they were kept clean. White was a Sunday colour in the 1920s and we wore a white lace pinafore and white broderie anglaise knickers which tied with bows below the knees. Gloves were worn, even in summer, and we always went out wearing a hat.

My mum went to the evening service at church and my sister and I went to Sunday school in the morning and afternoon. My other sister could not walk far enough to go because of her bad legs, and my father never went between marriage and death. We were allowed to go for a walk after Sunday school in the afternoon providing we kept clean but between classes we had Sunday lunch.

Sunday lunch meant roast beef, usually a big piece of sirloin. Mum made Yorkshire pudding and all the vegetables were grown on my Dad's "piece" and there were always plenty. Cabbage we seemed to have a lot, plus carrots and swede with a white sauce and occasionally parsley. The potatoes were available in bulk supply, often cooked with a dash of mint. After tea Mum would get herself ready for church and out came her shawl and best hat.'

◼ THE USUAL ROUTINE ◼

'When I was a little tot, in about 1945, I remember Sunday evenings well. The usual routine was to walk to Surprise View near the Royalty at Otley Chevin. I was allowed my special treat – a bottle of dandelion and burdock, or a lemonade and a bag of crisps (with the salt in a little blue bag). They were purchased from a house actually on Surprise View owned by a family called Jackson. One could walk through the front door and there was a little hatch where food and drink were sold.'

◙ Days I Hated ◙

'The late 1920s and early 1930s were the years that I hated. At that time my mother and I lived with my maternal grandmother who was a Wesleyan Methodist and the following is an example of a typical Sunday whilst living under her roof.

Sunday morning meant being dressed in my "Sunday best" clothes which were for Sundays only. At 10.30 am we all had to go to chapel. I didn't like going because the highly polished pews had hard cushions on them; these were stuffed with horse-hair which prickled mercilessly the parts of your legs below the short trousers we wore. It was a cardinal sin to sit in the wrong pew, the ones nearest the preacher were reserved for the gentry, millowners, shopowners, doctors, JPs etc. So much for our so called democracy; even in the eyes of God you were segregated – them and us! After listening to sermons about what would happen to you if you stepped out of line, or even asked Why? came the usual ritual of dropping a silver threepenny bit into the small red velvet "fishing" bag, followed by more hymns and readings, then at last the service came to an end. Then came the part I hated the most, the bowing and scraping, having to tip your cap to your so called "betters".

It was then time to go home and have Sunday dinner, which was the biggest meal of the week, Yorkshire pudding and onion gravy followed by roast beef, boiled and roast potatoes and two or three seasonal vegetables. After dinner we had to sit quietly and read the Bible. We were not allowed to play games or play out. In the afternoon the youngsters had to go to Sunday school. I hated this, especially in the summer when the sun would be shining and we were all closeted in a smelly old Sunday school room.

When I got older it was frowned upon to go out with a girl belonging to another denomination, ie a Baptist or Unitarian.

There were dropped voices of disapproval and even worse was if the girl was Church of England. There was a great deal of hostility towards you to try and get you to find a "good Wesleyan girl". It was also taboo to even think about going to any place of entertainment on a Sunday, these were considered to be places of the Devil.

Some people say, "Oh! the good old days!" Well, I lived through some of them and personally I'm glad they are gone and will soon be lost in the annals of history.'

◼ SUNDAY ◼

'Sunday always began with all the family sitting round the table to a full cooked breakfast. Then it was off to church in your Sunday best. Then home to dinner, when Dad always carved the meat. We had Yorkshire puddings with thick onion gravy first, separate from the meat and vegetables. My Mam always sprinkled a few currants in one corner of the pudding before she cooked it, this was her Sunday afternoon treat and nobody else was allowed to touch that bit of the pudding.

In the afternoon we were allowed to sit and read, sew or draw quietly but we were never allowed to play out with our friends.

Sunday afternoon tea was always ham or salmon sandwiches with tinned fruit and cream for afters and there was always a rich fruit, cherry or madeira cake to end the meal off perfectly. This was all helped down with plenty of strong milky tea.

In those days your Mam was always there to scold, nurse, listen, help and most of all love. In fact the home revolved around her and her work was never done.'

◼ MEMORABLE OCCASIONS ◼

'Each year at Netherton a prizegiving concert was held when children with a good Sunday school attendance would receive a prize, usually a book with a label stuck in front with the amount of marks you had amassed. Some years there was also a trip to the seaside and this was always looked forward to. Everyone would meet at chapel on the morning and then the coaches left

A Sunday school outing in the 1950s from Holbeck.

the village in convoy.

The harvest festival was another memorable occasion. Everyone would bring their own produce and the chapel would be decorated with vegetables, bread, fruit, sheaves of corn and flowers. On the Monday night following, all the produce would be auctioned and the proceeds put towards chapel funds.'

◙ THE SOCIAL CENTRE ◙

'The social centre of Chapelthorpe in the 1920s was the chapel. Concerts would be organised and sometimes a party from another chapel would come and put a concert on. There were faith teas, social evenings and bazaars, and the choir would sing Handel's *Messiah* at Christmas. Every Christmas Eve they went round the village singing carols, with a harmonium taken round on a wheelbarrow. On Good Friday there was a tea before the prizegiving, and once a year the chapel Anniversary when the children sat on the platform and sang hymns. That was when you got your new clothes. It always seemed to be hot in those days and many's the time you got your new dress marked with tar from the shoes of the person who sat behind you. Sadly in 1980 the chapel closed after 110 years.'

'In the 1940s I went to Armley Branch Road Methodist chapel, to the Sunday school. I went on all the Whitsuntide treats, usually to Farnley Park where we had a picnic and, after changing from our "Whitsy clothes" into something old, ran races. We always went there in a coach and sang songs all the way home.

I loved the concerts held in the chapel on Saturday night. We knew most of the performers. A boy called Barry Thewlis, who had been taught tap dancing at Miss Pinkney's Dancing School on Armley Town Street, nearly always gave a performance. I would sit and watch, entranced!

On Sundays we nearly always walked across Armley Park to my Grandma's for tea, where we would meet my aunt, uncle and cousins. Tea usually consisted of tongue, ham or brawn followed by prunes and custard and seed cake. In the evening the grown ups sat around Grandma's big table with a chenille cover and played cards for money. All Methodists too!'

▨ THE MOLLICARR SING ▨

'This annual event on Whit Sunday was first held in 1900. It was started by the Zion chapel, Almondbury, later amalgamated with the Wesleyan Methodist church and now simply the Methodist church. The walk always started at 7.30 am, mainly through the Mollicarr (mollis means kestrel, carr means wood), with the singing of hymns at allotted places through the walk. The woods were at their best, with new green foliage and birds in full song. The Sing finished about 9 am and in earlier years Mr and Mrs Gostridge of Farnley Hey boundary provided the breakfast – ham and eggs for the grown ups and bantam eggs for the children.'

▣ ONWARD CHRISTIAN SOLDIERS ▣

'In 1945 at the tender age of eight years I took part in a procession dressed in old-fashioned clothes and thought it great fun! We marched up the hill from our Sunday school at Horbury Bridge, a small village situated on the Huddersfield Road, about four miles from Wakefield. The significance of what I was doing eluded me at the time – namely retracing the footsteps of my great-grandmother, who was one of the children for whom the Rev Sabine Baring-Gould wrote the words of, arguably, the world's most famous hymn, *Onward Christian Soldiers*, 80 years previously in 1865.

We sang it to the tune by which it is best known today – *St Gertrude* by Sullivan and not the original tune from Haydn's Symphony in D number 15. I don't think many people in the Wakefield area are aware that this hymn was written for local children, but I shall always remember my small part in recreating its origin.'

▣ BENNY PARR ANNIVERSARY ▣

'Lady Ann Road, where I lived as a child, sticks out like a finger from near Batley station, into the countryside below Hawley Hall. Only one side of the road is fringed by houses. On the other side is a beck, securely fenced off from the road, but serving as an activity course for energetic children.

There the road ends, twin tracks fork: one climbing slowly at first to the farm, and then more steeply to the ruins of Hawley Hall, the other keeping fairly level, leading to Scotsman Lane.

Between the tracks lies a triangular piece of rising ground, which was the site used by Cambridge Street Independent Methodist church for the outdoor Anniversary service. This must have taken

place about June, to allow the evening service to be completed and the members of the congregation to reach home before dark.

Our first hint of the approach of this Anniversary was the invitation to some relations who were members of this church, to spend the interval between the afternoon and evening services at our house, and to enjoy high tea with us. From then we were on the *qui vive* for the arrival of the forms on which a goodly proportion of the church members would sit. These forms, piled and securely tied on flat carts, were pulled slowly along the road by sturdy horses, loaned, I should imagine, by some benevolent mill owner. A piano or organ was also carefully inserted into the load.

The three Anniversary services were all very well attended, by a congregation traditionally dressed in their newest and best finery. The weather, as far as I recall, was always fine and sunny. It was a fine sight to watch from the windows of our house, all the variety of style and colour of the unaccustomed crowds.

We enjoyed preparing for our afternoon visitors; the addition of a young girl and a boy toddler to our numbers gave an added fillip to our normal tea time. Afterwards we accompanied our guests to the evening service. We took up positions on the edge of the field, enjoying a sense of detachment from the sermon, but delighted with the singing in which we joined.

When the service was over, we were able to linger with our parents as they chatted to people they only met infrequently, and to watch with interest and regret the loading of the forms and the piano, denoting the end of this unusual occurrence until next year.'

▧ WONDERFUL DAYS ▧

'At Whitsuntide all the Sunday schools used to walk through the village, near Huddersfield, and sing at various street corners. They carried banners and the village band would play. Usually it was very hot and in those days the streets were repaired by being tarred and then pebbles or small stones put on the hot tar, so therefore as we stood singing, our sandals would stick to the tar and maybe it would get on my dress and if it did I got a good hiding. My mother used to put lard on the dress and try to get the mark out. Sometimes it worked, but sometimes not. After the walk and sing, we went to a field and were given tea and currant teacake and a bun and maybe a few monkey nuts. Then there were races. If it rained we had the tea in the Sunday school and it was always very noisy.

Once a year there was a bazaar at the Sunday school. I thought that was a wonderful day. Each class had a stall. The stalls were all decorated up and looked beautiful. I was given some money and could spend it on whatever I fancied. Each year too, there was a children's concert. A man came and taught all the children. He was rather strict, but I suppose he would have to be to make all the children do things properly. On Tuesday night there was a lantern lecture. Thinking back it was very primitive. Slides were put in a machine and a light or beam shone from the back of the room onto the slide. The boys used to shout and we used to chew bubble gum and blow bubbles. I would only be about eight years old and my friend and I had to walk home in the dark by ourselves.'

The early cars often became part of the family.

GETTING ABOUT

Trams and trolley buses, horses and cars, bicycles and motorbikes with sidecars – transport has changed a great deal over the years.

▣ FIRST CARS AND FULL BUSES ▣

'My grandfather told of seeing a first motor car in Keighley – someone came home from town and said that there was a motor car in the square and it was going to Manchester. Grandad and his mates ran two miles to the Manchester-Skipton Road to watch it go past.

My bedroom looked out over fields to the railway two miles

RIPPONDEN 97

*Ripponden & District Coaches were among those offering a more
comfortable ride for their passengers after the war.*

away. If I woke in the night I would often see the Thames-Clyde
Express with its two fire-breathing monster engines heading for
the Settle-Carlisle stretch. I loved the way their fires lit up the
night sky.

My uncle bought his first car about 1952/3. One day we were
going on an outing up Buck Haw Brow near Settle. If your car
engine would get you up there it was quite a feat in those days. On
our way up we passed a low loader (I'd never seen one before)
with Donald Campbell's *Blue Bird* on it – stuck halfway up the hill.
Donald was in the road directing traffic round it as they waited for
tractors to come to help them to the top of the hill. Perhaps it's a
pity they ever got up as he was killed two or three days later.

1911

City of Leeds.

2/6.

OMNIBUS DRIVER'S LICENCE.

No. *2/7*

THE LORD MAYOR, ALDERMEN, AND CITIZENS OF THE CITY OF LEEDS, acting by the COUNCIL, DO HEREBY LICENSE

James William White

residing at *23 Ingram Row Holbeck*

to act as the Driver of any Omnibus licensed to ply for hire within the said City, subject to, and in accordance with the Acts of Parliament and Bye-laws for time being in force.

This Licence is granted upon the condition that the Licensee so often as he changes his place of abode shall within two days thereof give notice in writing to the INSPECTOR OF HACKNEY CARRIAGES at his office, his new place of abode.

This Licence, unless otherwise revoked or suspended, shall continue and be in force until the Thirty-first day of March, One thousand nine hundred and *twenty four*

Dated this *first* day of *April* One thousand nine hundred and *twenty three*

R. E. Fox

Clerk of the Council.

NOTE.—This Licence is to be delivered to, and retained in the possession of, the Proprietor of the Omnibus while the Driver remains in his employ.

A Leeds omnibus driver's licence of 1923.

35

We went to senior school in the town and the bus home was always very full. The law was that no more than five people should stand in the aisle but the driver would let us pack in as there was an hour to wait for the next bus. Sometimes there was a policeman on point duty at the crossroads in the town centre and on these occasions the driver shouted, "Duck down, t'bobby's there" and we cowered in the aisle until out of sight. The bus was owned by a man in the village and had wooden slat seats – no upholstery at all. At busy times he employed a conductor to collect the fares, and the bus ran to his time – his pocket watch was *always* right. If it didn't correspond with the pips on the radio then the BBC was wrong!'

◼ A GREAT THRILL ◼

'The first motor car in Stocksmoor was an open tourer with a canvas top. It was owned by four men jointly and was known as "Wheel-apiece". One Sunday one of the sharers took my brother and me out for a ride. It was a great thrill. We were rounding a corner on a rough road and one of the wheels came off (I don't know whose it was!). We had to walk home from the Red Lion at Jackson Bridge back to Stocksmoor.'

◼ TANDEM AND SIDECAR ◼

'My parents were in the "Bramley Wheelers" tandem club. Father was the captain and used to organise paperchases and treasure hunts. They travelled all over the British Isles with camping equipment and clothes carried in panniers on the tandem.

After the war motorbikes were the fashion and as a little girl I had holidays to Scarborough and to relations in Devon (a two day journey) that I will always remember – Mum and me in the sidecar and Dad on the bike. We occasionally broke down but the AA man never seemed far away and always saluted us when seen on the road.'

The first 'Electric Car' or tram arrives at Horsforth in 1906.

▣ THE FIRST TRAM ▣

'The first tram arrived at Calverley Lane terminus in Horsforth at 8.15 am on 16th May 1906; the driver was Mr Annakin and my great uncle was the conductor.'

▣ BUSES AND TRAMS ▣

'Because I went to the high school in Lawnswood we had to go on a bus from the top of Broadgate Lane. At first we had to walk about half a mile to catch the bus at about 8.20 am but later a little bus ran from the Glenroyal cinema to the Old Ball and this was timed to link with the bus through Headingley to Leeds, which only ran once each hour. In the early days, on this route a firm called G. F. Tate ran a really dilapidated bus, alternating with the West Yorkshire Road Car Co.

Returning from school at 4 pm we caught the bus which came from Leeds and sometimes was rather full of shoppers by the time it got to West Park, but however full the bus was, one particular conductor always crammed us all on. We sat on each other's knees and on our cases in the gangway; officially only five were allowed to stand. Our behaviour was illegal and one day the police were waiting for us (obviously having been tipped off). Two officers jumped out from the hedge on Butcher Hill and stopped the bus; the conductor shouted, "Sit on the floor", so we all tried to hide since the police only gave a cursory look from the door. I often wonder if that kindhearted conductor was fined. I'm sorry to say, after that we sometimes had to walk down Spen Lane to Kirkstall Abbey to catch the tram which ran to Guiseley.

The tram ran from Roundhay Park through Leeds and up to Guiseley; the fare was 3d from Leeds to Guiseley.'

▩ ON THE 'TRACKLESS' ▩

'I used to travel to junior school at Manningham on a trolley bus or "trackless" as they were called, this relating back to the days when the buses did actually run on tracks. The trolleys were hooked onto overhead cables by two long poles from the top of the bus, and it was a great delight to us when these slipped off and the bus ground to a halt. This happened quite often, as school was at the terminus where the turning circle was quite tight; the poles having no flexibility frequently pulled off. The conductor then had to rush out with an extremely long rod which was used to push the connectors back onto the cables. At this time I was also madly in love with the bus conductor who was regularly on my bus.'

▩ A CITY CHILD ▩

'I'm a city child, born and bred in Bradford, so my memories are of trams and trolley buses, high-piled huge bales of wool on carts pulled by horses with feathered feet and polished brasses. I remember when Town Hall Square was paved with wooden setts, and being taken into the town to see the shop windows illuminated for the first time after the dark days of the Second World War.

Outings were few but one favourite was to Saltaire and Shipley Glen; not to be undertaken without a bit of forward planning because it involved two bus journeys. First, we crossed the field behind our house and over the road to the bus stop. The journey took longer if the connecting trolley came off its overhead wire. Then we all waited patiently until the driver and conductor laboriously pulled a long, long pole from its special storage place underneath the bus and used it to persuade the fitting back onto the wires.

Then another bus ride from the centre of Bradford, along Manningham Lane (passing Busby's store – the best Father Christmas Grotto in Bradford) and out to Saltaire. Then the descending road of the model village itself. I remember the stone lions and the lovely church. I was told that the lions were left over from Trafalgar Square. The houses were where Titus Salt's workers lived, but they were not allowed to sit out at the front or hang out washing. Past the enormous mill, then up a short climb to the highlight of the trip – a ride on the Glen Tramway. It was best of all at bluebell time, when the scent was heavenly. The open "carriages" had no sides or roof and the bare wooden seats had moveable backs, so that you could face up or down. The rising tram was pulled up by the descending one by means of a cable and the two passed halfway up the hill. At the top was a little street of cottages and all the inhabitants seemed to have diversified (before that word was invented). One sold bunches of flowers, another cups of tea. One had a mini fair and another a little boat on a tiny pond, round a central rock. Best of all was the thrilling chair ride, out over the long drop to the grass below, on chairs hanging from overhead tracks, round in a loop and back again.

We could rarely afford even a cup of tea (taking sandwiches and lemonade with us) and sometimes not even a ride on the tramway but a brief venture out onto the moor beyond the little houses and then home again. The pull up the hill past the model village was hard on young legs – I expect if I went back the pull would be equally hard on my old legs!'

HOUSE & HOME

The Way We Lived Then

'*N*ice *as it is to reminisce about the good old days, I, for one, do not want to go back to them.' It is a sentiment many of us would agree with, as we look back to the days when lighting was by candle, oil or gas, heating came only from the fire or range, and our houses were often cramped and crowded!*

▧ Holidays on the Farm ▧

'My mother, born in 1900, was a farmer's daughter, the youngest of four children, and some of my earliest memories are of holidays on the farm in Yorkshire. That gorgeous smell of baking as soon as we opened the door; there was always bread rising by the blackleaded fireplace and the kettle on the hob. Granny's Yorkshire tea cakes were the best I have ever tasted.

It must have been a hard life as there was no mains water, it came from a pump in the yard. The privy was across the yard, with two wooden seats side by side, a place to be visited only when absolutely necessary as we never knew what we might encounter; perhaps a kitten might be curled up on the lid, an odd mouse might run across from the barn nearby, or we might be visited by one of the hens, they really were free range.

The best bit was staying the night, going up the wooden stairs with our candle or oil lamp, getting undressed, usually in a freezing cold bedroom, standing on the rag rug, then jumping into that lovely feather bed. It was often warm as Granny had been up with the warming pan or sometimes we had a stone hot water bottle. My sister and I both slid to the middle of the bed as it was so soft, but so very cosy.

In the morning a great treat was to help with the milking, then take the buckets of warm frothy milk to the dairy to put through the separator. We sometimes got to lick the last drops of cream out of the bowl – delicious. I remember watching Granny making butter in the churn then patting it into shape with wooden paddles and wrapping it in muslin ready for market.

Sometimes we were allowed in the front room at the farm – I never saw it used. Everyone lived in the huge kitchen, a cosy room where a fire burned in the grate all the year round as that was the only means of cooking with the oven at the side. There was a huge scrubbed table in the middle of the room which was covered by a chenille cloth when it wasn't in use. There were rocking chairs by the fire, although I don't remember them being used very often, Granny was always busy. There always seemed to be geraniums on the window sill. The front room had a polished table with some waxed fruit under a glass dome in the middle. The chairs were pushed back around the room and I remember a rather uncomfortable horsehair sofa.'

▨ Our First House ▨

'Our first 17 years of married life were hard, in a rented house at Chapelthorpe, eleven shillings a week rent and no labour saving devices. We had coconut matting on the kitchen floor, with newspapers underneath to catch the dirt, and "candles to light you to bed", the house having no electricity. My life changed when we moved, and I now enjoy easier living with electric devices and central heating. Nice as it is to reminisce about the good old days, I, for one, do not want to go back to them.'

▨ Pit Row ▨

'A row of houses not far across the fields from us at Roberttown was called Pit Row. In the end one lived a brother and sister. He was a coal miner and every month he had a tipper lorry sent from the pit with his ration of free coal. It was just tipped onto the dirt street by the coal hole in the flags outside his house. My friends and I used to pick all the slate out and throw the large lumps of coal down the coal hole. We were given a penny to share for sweets.'

On a park bench in 1921 at Purston, near Pontefract.

❖ BLUBBERHOUSES HALL ❖

'My uncle was the estate agent for Leeds City waterworks. This meant he had a house provided; it was Blubberhouses Hall, a lovely house but cold, with stone-flagged passages. My sister and I used to love to go and stay with them, even though the loo was an Elsan chemical one, halfway up the stairs. There was a bathroom, however, with bath and running water! No tin bath in front of the fire and probably one of the few in the village.

My aunt cooked in the oven next to the fire, this was still the norm in towns as well as the country and continued for many years; the forerunner of the Aga. We often wonder today how they judged and controlled the temperature, I don't remember any burnt offerings. To boil a kettle meant lighting a methylated spirit stove and pumping it to keep it going, in her hands very

*Wedding parties, at Stanbury in the early 1900s and in Holbeck in
1959, show how much our lives have changed.*

efficient. I remember her once sending me down to the village shop to get some paraffin and old Mrs S was having her lunch and wasn't at all pleased to have to pour out paraffin into the can I had taken. Another time I went for some bottles of lemonade, the sort with a glass marble as a stopper. Mrs S didn't recognise me and thinking I was only passing through told me that there was a penny back on the bottle; a privilege denied my cousins.

I cannot remember how the house was lit after dark, I don't remember having a candle or paraffin lamp. I think a generator had been installed in the river Washburn and this produced enough electricity to be able to have lights energised by electricity, but not power.'

▓ LIFE IN CUTSYKE IN THE 1920S ▓

'We children ate at the large oval table in the front room and our parents ate in the kitchen so that Mum could watch her oven. No talking was allowed at meal times and we always ate whatever was on the plate in front of us. The mahogany table was usually covered with a dark red cloth with a pompom fringe which hung halfway to the ground and hid the legs. A second cloth was added before each meal – coloured on weekdays but white on Sundays. The second cover kept the first clean so that it could be kept permanently in place protecting the table. The large bulbous legs were wrapped in thick wool stockings held by elastic at the top to prevent the children kicking the legs when sat at the table. The stockings were removed on Sundays when the legs shone beautifully and then they were covered again for the week. The matching sideboard stretched almost to the ceiling with a large oval mirror and barley twist supports holding small shelves with ornaments displayed. There were two large drawers and cupboards below and in the centre smaller cupboard, Mum kept her best black velour hat.

Also in the front room was a black horsehair sofa which prickled your legs if not protected by a long skirt. Also two black armchairs for Mum and Dad's use only, woe betide anyone else who was found sitting there. When the chairs were pulled up to the fire in the evening it was too bad for those sitting behind.

Miners' cottages were built around blazing coal fires and once cut off from the heat the stone floors and ill-fitting doors made it impossible to keep warm.

Under the window was a small table with a cloth and a large aspidistra. The only time the plant moved was when it rained and Mum put it outside the back door for a good soak. Like all the furniture, the aspidistra was polished every week – each leaf being rubbed with a drop of milk, so that the fat from the cream would add to the shine. Each child had their own jobs but I was the first reserve whenever the need for a substitute arose. George always did the outside duties – chopping wood and running errands and when he had to go to Castleford he would run each way usually with an iron hoop with which he kept pace.

Everything was cooked on the great coal fire or in the coal oven which was alongside. The fire itself was held back by six iron bars and a further three bars could hinge down over the burning coals to support the frying pan. Other pans were thrust into the fire with only the top bar for support and their long handles protruded forwards into the room. Like the fireplace itself, all the utensils were made of cast iron and were very heavy.

Every weekday we made bread – a stone of flour made eight big loaves and twice as much was made on Fridays. When I had learnt how to do it, I would get on with the first batch while my Mum made the sweet dough for bun loaf. We children ate bun loaf only on Sundays when it was regarded as a special treat but Dad took a fruit loaf down the pit as his "snap". Every day as the oven cooled we put in a big 15 inch square tin of gingerbread. This was suitable to take down the pit and we children were allowed a taste of this luxury. Mum would often send a piece to my aunt who was very partial to it.

It was the fireplace which was the showpiece and demonstrated to neighbours that you looked after your home. Every Friday the great range of ironwork was blackleaded and polished until it gleamed. Another weekly chore was flue cleaning which was necessary for the oven to heat properly otherwise the bread would not be right. So every week, I would be down on my knees, with my hair wrapped in a scarf and a harding apron made from an old sack protecting my dress, working up blisters on my hands, thrusting and twisting the big, stiff bottle brush into the narrow gap between the oven and the iron base plate and shovelling soot until there was no more.

Chimney sweeping was carried out by a dark-skinned man who always appeared on the first Monday of the new year. He was a very tidy man who cleaned up every scrap of soot which he carried away in his cart. The soot was used as a fertiliser by the local farmer.

In front of the range was a brass-topped fireguard, a brass-handled iron kettle and a hearth set of brush, shovel and tongs – all with long brass handles. Beyond this was the fender – again, in burnished brass and all needing a weekly workover with Brasso. My Mum would never let me do the daily task of cleaning the lamps, considering the combination of paraffin lamps and a blazing fire to be too dangerous for even the most careful and willing of children. She also insisted on purchasing the paraffin and carrying it from the village herself. She was very proud of her lamps which, apart from the blazing fire, were our only source of light in the days before electricity. Her favourite was the big lamp which stood in the centre of the table in our living room and was much admired by all who saw it. It was over two feet tall and cast a creamy-white glow when it burned, which illuminated the whole room. It had a cast iron base and an assortment of glass fitments, all of which attracted smoky deposits from the burning paraffin. Every morning Mum collected all the lamps together and washed the blackened glass with soapy water until the sparkle returned. Then she trimmed the wicks, refilled the reservoirs with paraffin and replaced the lamps ready for lighting in the evening.'

❖ WHITLEY WILLOWS ❖

'The water was pumped from the pit into the beck but they depended on it, even though it was red with rust and nothing lived in it! Lighting for the house and power was generated from it, and Whitley Willows became the first house in the district to have electricity.

My grandparents and family lived in the cottage in two thirds of an acre of land, by the stream and near my grandfather's workplace. He was the engineer, responsible for all the steam, power and gas being ready for the workers to start at 7.30 am.

As his day began at 5 am most of the year it was dark and an oil lamp was difficult. At first he generated electricity to give him light from the mill engine. This triggered off the idea to illuminate his own home, with the stream the source of energy.

The culvert into the dam ran higher than the stream so from this he piped water down to a waterwheel and dynamo, this generated electricity. It was then wired across to the garage and stored in accumulators. Lights were wired into all rooms, and the cellar had a switch to turn off the light when you closed the door, so that the light was not left on!

Then on his pedal lathe he made and wound motors to drive the mangle, the gramophone, and later to drive both his lathe and a wireless.

At 60 after a heart worry he was advised to retire before pension age. So the family agreed to give extra contributions to fund the running of the home. Now he could devote all his time to "knackling", as he called it!

He was lame from polio and wore a calliper on one leg, but this did not deter his love of cricket. Batting was his strong contribution, and he was allowed a runner with his disability. Even with limited finances the household was always buzzing with friends and they could always make up a cricket team on weekends in the summer. His brother Billy captained England at cricket and shared many hours playing billiards with my grandfather.

I have many happy memories of Whitley Willows but sadly it is no longer. Now only the weeping willow tree and two fruit trees remain in what is now a car park.'

▨ MY GRANDMOTHER'S HOUSE ▨

'I was born in 1929 in my grandmother's house, in a remote hamlet between Blackmoorfoot and Slaithwaite.

If I shut my eyes I can see seven or eight houses built around a yard. At the bottom of the yard was a scrapyard owned by a family called Schofield, I think that also all the houses were owned by them. J. B. Schofield I don't remember, and I think he must have died, but I do remember "Mrs JB", as she was known to all of us. It was like an extended family there, as there was Norman (JB's son) and "Mrs Norman", and Jack Hodgson the lorry driver, and "Mrs Jack". For years I thought "Jack" was her surname.

Our house was a big draughty place with a flagged floor, with bright rag rugs made by Grandma. A big fire burned in the kitchen range. The only other light was from gas lamps, downstairs. We went to bed by candlelight. The radio, Dad's pride and joy, was powered by an acid battery which had to be charged regularly. Before that, he had a home-made crystal set.

The earth toilet was in an outhouse, and quite a trek from the house. Mum was afraid to go down there in the dark without Dad standing guard. In each toilet there was a board with a row of three holes cut in it, all different sizes. Mine was the smallest. Some poor man from the council came regularly to empty them. Water came from a well in the yard; Dad made a cover for this so I wouldn't fall in.

We lived at 5 Greenhead until I was four years old, and I have happy memories of a life spent in a refuge shut away from the outside world. I thought it was the whole world. I was the only young child living there and I went in and out of all the houses, sure of a welcome everywhere.

My Grandma, a devout churchgoer and a member of the Mothers' Union, had very strict rules in the home. On Sundays we were not allowed to do any unnecessary work. Any missing buttons or darning must wait until Monday, even if we had to get up extra early to do it. We weren't allowed to play cards at any time.

For a time, when I was little, my mother worked in a textile mill and Grandma looked after me. I used to help her with the dusting, rubbing hard at the table legs, which had old socks over them during the week to protect them from scratches.

When she did the housework she donned a sacking or "harding" apron over her usual pinafore, and she wore a dustcap.

Monday was washday, Tuesday for ironing and airing the clean clothes, Wednesday was baking day. Grandma was up bright and early to light the fire and get the flames roaring under the oven. She kneaded all the bread and put it by the fire to rise, covered with a clean tea towel. There were loaves, teacakes, and currant teacakes filling the house with a wonderful smell. Then she made pastry. There was always a meat and potato pie for tea that night, and apple pies, custard pies, jam tarts and my grey thimble cakes. There was also a slab of pastry baked on a tray. This was called "fatcake" and Dad loved it hot from the oven with butter or jam on it. It wasn't the healthiest thing to eat, but neither was the beef dripping he loved to eat on his bread! After all this she always made two fruit loaves and two sponge cakes. I don't know how she managed all this in one day. She must have been exhausted.

Next day, the fireplace had to be blackleaded and rubbed until it shone, ready for the weekend when she would sit in her rocking chair by the fire. I would rock beside her in my own small chair and we would play our favourite game of looking for pictures in the glowing coals. We used to get salesmen and gypsies around there, and one time, after they'd left, my big coloured ball was missing from the yard. "They'll be playing catch as they go over the hill," said Grandma. "It'll help them on their way".'

▨ Pudsey Memories ▨

'My memories of home conditions in the late 1920s would probably sound terrible to the children of today and possibly their parents too.

Most houses in Pudsey were terraced type cottages, with stone-floored living room, a stone sink at the top of the cellar steps, or the "cellar head" as it was known, with just one tap, cold water of course and a bucket below the sink to catch the waste water.

Cooking was usually done on two gas rings or if you were a bit posh, a proper gas cooker. This was in addition to a cast-iron fireplace which had a hob in the middle, an oven usually on the right-hand side with hot water container on the left, both of them being heated from the fire.

Making the fire in the morning was a real chore as the ashes and dust from the previous day's fire had to be cleaned out and the new fire had to be laid with newspapers screwed up with wooden chips on top plus some of the old cinders and some coal.

The bedroom was up a flight of stone steps, Mam and Dad had an iron-framed double bed and the children then slept in the same room, quite often a number of children to the same bed. I know of one family where the parents had seven children and they lived in two rooms (a one-up and one-down house). The parents had a bed and all the children slept in another bed in the same room as their parents.

For the night toilet an enamel pail with a lid was used and when I was very young I remember a timber cart used to come round and collect the "night soil". The toilet used during the day was usually situated at the end of the street and shared between two or three families; in the same yard was the midden which was like a small stable and was where all the rubbish was disposed of, and then collected once a week. As you can imagine, in the summer the smell was strong, to say the least.'

▨ Rugs and Rhoda ▨

'Friday was cleaning day. All the brasses had to be cleaned and polished – a brass fender, a stand with poker, tongs and shovel, brass candlesticks and brass stair rods. The fireplace itself was blackleaded. All the rugs were taken outside and given a good shake, and the flagstones, windowsills and steps were scrubbed on hands and knees and the edges "ruddled". The ruddle-stone was soft yellow/brown stone bought from a woman who came round once a week and was known to all as "Ruddle Rhoda". The outside toilet was washed and scrubbed, and the stone floor was rubbed with "donkey stone". Squares of newspaper cut into six inch squares were threaded on a string and hung behind the door. If you got a job cleaning someone's toilet to earn extra money, you got sixpence!

On winter evenings the whole family would help to make a

new "prodded" rug. Canvas or sacking was stretched on a wooden frame. All the old woollen garments which had been discarded during the previous year were saved and these were cut into strips an inch wide and three inches long, called "lists", which were stored in carrier bags according to colour. Using a wooden skewer, a hole was made in the canvas and a list pushed halfway through, then another hole was made and the other half of the list pulled through that. Different districts had their own individual patterns; ours was a six-inch black border with a scarlet diamond in the middle. The scarlet material was damaged "ends" from the cloth made for soldiers' uniforms. The space between the border and the diamond was filled with assorted pieces. The rug had to be finished in time to have a new hearthrug for Christmas, and the old one was relegated to some other part of the room.'

▣ First Impressions ▣

'My first impression was gained on a visit to my new in-laws to be. I came by train to Leeds where I was met by my future husband and then we took the bus to Halifax. As we approached the brow of a hill into Halifax, nothing had prepared me for the sight before me. We were sitting in the upstairs front seat of the bus. Spread out before me were more mill chimneys than I had ever seen in my life. All the buildings were black, even the trees and small areas of grass were black and the air was dense with smoke. However, the house that my future husband had found for us was about three miles out of town in a quiet and pleasant cul-de-sac and aptly named Nursery Avenue – since we were to have three children in the next four and a half years. In the eleven years we lived there, there was always at least one new baby in a pram outside someone's front door – not bad for 26 houses.'

WATER AND WASHDAY

No mod cons meant no running water and no mains sewerage, and that meant fetching every drop of water from the pump or well, earth closets at the bottom of the garden, bath night in front of the fire, and – the bane of housewives' lives – that all day drudgery of washday.

PUMPS AND WELLS

'Prior to 1920 in Stocksmoor, all household water was obtained from pumps in the yards or carried from local wells when the springs dried up. We were the first family in the village to have water piped into the house, and a neighbour had the first upstairs bathroom. It had a bath and washbasin but all the water used in it had to be hand pumped from the kitchen sink downstairs.'

'In the 1920s we lived in East Hardwick. We had to carry our water from the pump across the road. It was good drinking water but too hard for washing ourselves and our clothes. We caught rainwater from the roof and after filtering it, used it for washing as it was so much softer.'

FROM THE SPRING

'As a child in the 1930s I lived in the Holme Valley at Honley. How well I remember having to carry water from the standpipes in hot weather as our well was dry, but for drinking we had to walk half a mile for spring water from the wood. We had never had corporation water and nobody would drink it.'

'The house where I was born was an old stone one, surrounded by fields and a good half hour's walk from the nearest village. Our water supply was from a trough in the corner of the kitchen fed by spring water which ran beneath the house. It was pure and cold.'

▨ BATH NIGHT ▨

'Although we had a bath in the attic, in winter it was just too cold at the top of the house to be of any use. Then the tin bath was brought up from the cellar and placed in front of the coal fire and filled with kettles of hot water from the kitchen stove. What a laborious job it was emptying the bath after the whole family had used the water. The dirty water had to be poured into buckets and disposed of down the sink.'

'Friday night was bath night. Children were bathed first, then dressed in nighties and given "pobbies" (bread soaked in hot milk) for supper and sent to bed. Mum and Dad then added more hot water to the bath to warm it up and had their own baths. If a family had a dog, it got bathed last!'

▨ IT WASN'T EASY ▨

'Forty five years ago when my husband and I were married at 20 years of age, we bought a stone cottage at the end of a terrace in Yeadon. It cost us £200, which was Owen's inheritance when his Mum died. Our home was a one-up, one-down with an attic full of woodworm. We had a stone flagged floor, a fireplace which needed blackleading, one cold water tap in a sink under a

cupboard, and one gas ring. We shared an outside toilet in the backyard with our neighbour. Bathtime meant bringing the gas boiler in from the old wash house and taking the tin bath from the wall and shaking out a spider or two. Then getting dressed after the bath and going out and emptying it down the drain in the yard.

One day while I was at work and Owen was on leave from the army he decided to have a bath. He got the water nicely hot in the gas boiler and went for the bath. When he saw the cobwebs he decided just to have a stand-up wash in the gas boiler. Luckily he was quite slim and fitted in easily – but it was very hot for his feet having the gas ring underneath!

A few years later when our two sons were four years and 18 months old I was washing. Having only one room I made a barricade so they could not reach the washer. But Graham (always a rascal) crawled through and pulled the gas-pipe off. John shouted, "Nasty smell, Mummy", which was lucky for me because I have no sense of smell. After that we bought an electric washer for safety.

Soon after, we moved into another terraced house but now we had a bath with big feet, a toilet in there with a high flush and three bedrooms – this was pure luxury and the good life at last. But we often laugh with our memories of our first home.'

'Friday nights were special. Before my husband went on his night out with the boys he trotted into the cellar and brought up a large wooden board. This was followed by the gas boiler, a dilapidated zinc affair, which was duly placed on the board, filled and lighted.

Tonight was bath night. If we were flush hubby would return with a fried fish each for supper. Then began the business of getting the water into the tin bath waiting on the rug in front of the fire. Clouds of steam (which did nothing for the wallpaper) arose, but it was all part of the ritual. The adage "ladies first" was the pattern and in I went, after tentatively testing the water with my big toe. Pink and glowing out I would get and after towelling dry put on the nightie warming in the coal oven. This was bliss in winter time.

In would go hubby, invariably oohing at the temperature of the water. Dried and pyjamad the emptying of the bath began. Poor hubby getting out the water with the lading can (the what? my children ask), huffing and puffing till the last drop was gone and, as on every Friday night he would say, "That takes all the pleasure out of getting bathed." Off to bed we would go secure in the knowledge that we were clean all over. Twenties? Thirties? No, this was the early 1950s and when two babies became part of the family, a kettle and pan heated on a double gas ring provided enough water for the baby bath and the water for nappy washing was heated the same way. No disposable nappies then. How, I wonder, did we cope? But we did, as did hundreds if not thousands like us and we were happy in spite of all the difficulties.'

◼ WASHDAY ◼

'In the 1930s Monday was always washday. This meant an early start and took all day. First the set-pot had to be filled with cold water, then a coal fire was lit in a grate underneath. This had a little door on hinges. The set-pot itself was like a cauldron set into bricks; it had a round wooden lid, and when not in use it had a wooden top and front which concealed the bricks and fire grate for the rest of the week.

The best white sheets and pillowcases and the linen tablecloths went in first, to be boiled. After some time the clothes were taken out with a truncheon-like stick called a "peggy stick", and they were dumped into a zinc wash tub and rinsed in cold water to which a "dolly-blue bag" had been dangled to make the water blue. This gave the clothes a lovely white tint as they dried. Before they were pegged out on the line they were rolled through a wooden mangle to squeeze out the excess water. The rest of the water from the set-pot was ladled into the tub and used to wash the coloured clothes, which were agitated with a "posser stick", a long stick like a broom handle with a bell-shaped metal end with holes in. Lastly, in went the greasy overalls my father wore all week at the mill.

Early evening the ironing was started. The solid irons were put

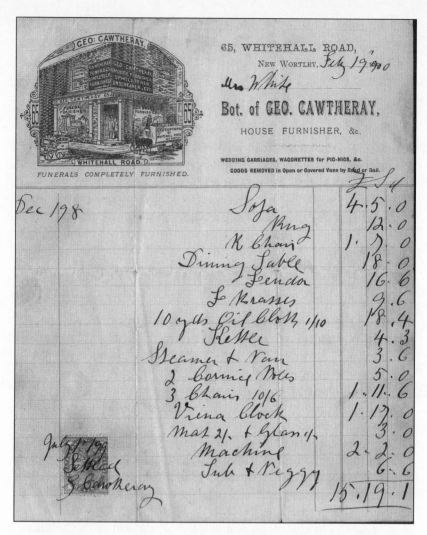

Setting up home in 1900 – from the sofa to the 'tub and peggy'.

on the coal fire to get really hot. You had to spit on them, and if it bounced off you knew they were hot enough. Later irons had a conical shape, and you filled them with charcoal. You opened a small hinged door and blew and blew until the charcoal got going and glowed red. There was a little chimney to let out the fumes. It's amazing that there were not more accidents on wash days!'

'Nobody ever washed on a Good Friday. It was someone's shroud you were washing.'

▨ DOWN TO THE PRIVY ▨

'Our toilets at Birdsedge in the 1920s were outside and most of them were earth closets. Some people had to walk a long way, around spooky corners, and when it was dark older brothers had to take the younger ones.'

'We lived in the 1950s in a small terraced house, one up and one down, which had originally been part of a public house. We had a large flagstoned living room, covered by rag rugs on the floor and with a huge blackleaded range. In one corner of the room was a trapdoor and this was the only way down to the cellar and the outside toilet, which we shared with other families. My mother used to panic every time she needed to go downstairs to the toilet because she had to leave the trapdoor open so she could get back in and she was afraid I would fall down. My mother paid a grand total of 3s 6d a week rent for that house.'

'Our old toilet was in the corner of a big yard, just a wooden seat with a hole in, no lid on. I went one night in the dark and sat down, and there was a squawking and thrashing of wings. I had sat on a broody old hen.

There were no doors on the big square midden, just a low two foot wall round, and in summer it was full of flies. We used to look up the tunnel and watch folk sat on the seat.'

'As a child living in Armley in the 1930s, I remember the lavatory up the street and the huge key on a wood bobbin. Sometimes our trips were torchlit, sometimes candlelit.'

'I was born in 1925 on a farm not more than three miles from the centre of Leeds. This was owned by the Middleton Estate & Colliery Company, who owned the colliery and a number of farms in the Middleton area.

Our main toilet was outside in the paddock. This was a dry

toilet with a wooden seat and central hole, with the usual newspaper hanging on the wall. Men came with a horse and cart to empty it. A commode and chamberpots were in the house for night time use. It was only when my brother caught diphtheria, with many complications, in the mid 1930s that we had water toilets put in the bathroom.'

FOOD AND SHOPPING

The delicious aromas of baking day remain an evocative memory of the past, when most food we ate was home cooked and very traditional.

◧ BAKING DAY ◧

'Wednesday was always baking day and my mother baked bread, tea cakes and sweet cakes. Oh! what a lovely smell, I can almost smell it now. The baked bread was put on a clean towel in the doorway to cool, and there was always new bread and butter for supper.

Dinner on baking day was always either meat and potato pie or "fry" which consisted of liver, kidney, heart, sweetbread and onions all done in a big dish in the oven at the side of the fire. The fire was built up and the end iron taken out, the damper was pulled out and then the fire went right under the oven. Yorkshire puddings, vegetables and potatoes accompanied the "fry" and there was usually a rice pudding to follow. What happy days.'

◧ IN THE KITCHEN ◧

'Special days for brewing, and a special day for putting surplus eggs into waterglass. Buckets of lime could be bought for twopence – diluted with water and a blue bag it was used to whitewash the kitchen, cellar, closet, and hen huts. Raspberry vinegar, elderberry syrup, jars of brimstone and treacle, lemon barley water, jars of goose grease, and ginger cordial were made and stored in the corner cupboard ready for winter use. Any spare sour milk was tied up and salted in a piece of fine cotton and hung outside to make cream cheese. All kinds of herbs were dried, then rubbed and sieved and stored in stone jars. Some were used in cooking, some made into a kind of pot pourri – lavender was tied in bunches or made into lavender bags and put into drawers, chests and wardrobes.

Sacks of potatoes were ordered and paid for, then delivered by horse and cart and a sack of turnips given free. Some farmers allowed their milk customers to go into the fields after the grain was harvested to collect gleanings to feed to the hens.

Empty sugar sacks were bought from the Co-op for 2d, but you had to go on a list and wait your turn – then they were unpicked and washed and cut into four, stitched round and made into harding towels. These were used to dry your hands on or as oven cloths or tucked into the tops of bread crocks to keep the bread moist and prevent it from going dry. Empty jam jars were returned and you were given ½d each. Bundles of newspapers were taken to the chip shop and you were given a bag of chips with bits on. Save twelve wrappers from Co-op Towel Soap and you could exchange them for a good sized striped towel, eight wrappers from Silver Seal margarine and you got a block of dark chocolate. A penny would buy an orange rope from the greengrocer and made two good skipping ropes.'

▩ KEEPING A PIG ▩

'My Dad had a smallholding and grew all his own vegetables, raised chickens for eggs and the occasional boiling fowl and also kept pigs. He grew a lot of potatoes, which was our staple diet along with kale, cauliflowers, red and green cabbage, turnips, beetroot, carrots, parsnips, peas and broad beans. There were no flowers as he wouldn't "waste ground growing them". There were great clumps of rhubarb which was forced under rusty buckets. He grew large onions and carefully wrapped each celery plant in newspaper as it grew to preserve the white stems.

My Dad was the only miner in the village to keep pigs but some of the people in Cutsyke gave scraps of food for them, thus making themselves eligible to place an order for pork at Christmas. Every day Dad and my brother George each carried a bucket of waste food down to the "piece" where the pigs were housed. On the way home from school my friend Hilda and I would stop at the "piece" and light a fire under the set-pot in which the pigs' feed would be boiled. Sometimes there was a sack of pig potatoes to add to the swill. My friend and I often cooked a potato each for ourselves on the end of a stick thrust into the fire. Dad kept just one mother pig and she produced a litter of pigs every year – as many as 17 piglets in one litter but then the mother invariably rolled on her offspring and crushed some. The piglets were weaned and sold off keeping just one pig for killing at Christmas and this was done "down the piece".

My Dad acted as slaughterman and butcher and Mum kept a book listing the neighbours' orders. The pig met its end on or just before 23rd December when Dad usually worked a morning shift at the pit giving him the afternoon and evening to cut up the pig. Neighbours arrived by appointment to collect their share and "cash on the nail" was the order of the day. My Dad would not sell the hams – these would be salted down in wooden boxes before wrapping in butter muslin and hanging in our kitchen. The hams kept the large iron frying pans in slices of meat for months to come but I never tasted it or my Mum as "ham was for the workers".'

'Most people at Chapelthorpe in the 1920s kept a pig, fed from kitchen scraps. Potato peelings were boiled up in an old oven and mixed with meal. It was jolly hard work when the pig was killed and the bacon and ham had to be cured. The salt used was bought in a block and had to be grated. There were sausages, brawn, scratchings and pork pies to be made, and pure lard rendered down from the leaf. The only thing not used in a pig was its squeak. The kids used to blow the bladder up and kick it about as a football.'

'Pig killing time was always a great time on our farm at the top of

Norwood Edge in the 1940s. There would be lots of tasty things to eat. I never taste pork these days like we had then, and those huge hams and sides of bacon were wonderful – if a little fatty. After all, the pig would be a few years old and probably weighed 40 stones.'

▨ AT THE CO-OP ▨

'Our shopping was done at the Co-op in Dewsbury. All the goods had to be weighed out, sugar put into blue bags, best flour into white bags, and the second quality into brown. The flour dropped down a shute from an upstairs room into large wooden bins. Most families had their own flour "pokes", heavy linen bags the size of a pillowcase, which were filled in your presence to make sure none of the cheaper quality was mixed in. Groceries were delivered to your home later in the day.'

'Thursday was shopping and market day. The shops were always full of tempting goods and you could get anything from a pin to periodicals on the market in Holmfirth. The greengrocer used to give the children an apple or an orange. But I was different, I always asked for a tomato instead, so a tomato I had.

We used to go to the Co-op and if you bought treacle it was weighed out into your own jar. You could buy Ceylon tea in little silver packets. Butter, lard and cheese were all cut off big blocks and wrapped up in greaseproof paper, white sugar, rice and other dry goods were weighed out and then put into thick blue paper bags with the tops folded in just so. Ham was cut from a big joint with the bone in; the grocer used a knife which seemed to me, at four years old, to be three foot long and so sharp it went through the ham as if it was butter. Bacon was sliced from a long piece on the big red and silver bacon slicing machine.

Biscuits were all sold loose out of big square tins with glass lids. I can remember my mother getting twopence worth as a treat when my aunt was coming for tea; my favourite ones were always garibaldi.

The grocer and his assistants all wore white smocks and stiff white aprons and the young boy who worked there wore a

The shop at Haggate Nook, Scartop, owned in the early years of the century by William Greenwood who sold everything from groceries to animal feed. In the 1920s it was taken over by Fred Jackson, and developed to provide teas.

brown overall; it was his job to do the sweeping up both inside and out and deliver groceries on his rickety old bicycle with the big basket on the front.'

▣ DELIVERED TO THE DOOR ▣

'At Dalton, Huddersfield in the 1930s shopping was a much easier job than it is today, in one respect at least, because most of it was delivered to the door. On Tuesday the fish man came, on Wednesday the butcher who took an order for Saturday delivery, on Thursday the greengrocer with his horse and cart, and on Friday the grocer. Milk and bread came daily. My mother went to town once a week.'

▣ TOWN AND VILLAGE SHOPS ▣

'Netherton had two fish and chip shops, two branches of the Middletown Co-operative Society, a post office, three general grocery shops, and a cobbler – Mr Bowers who came to the village each day from Horbury.

The main shops for groceries such as butter, sugar, flour etc were the Co-operative stores, where during the war some foods that were really scarce would be kept under the counter. Milk was delivered to the door in churns and the milkman had different sized ladles to transfer the milk straight to your jug.

One shop in the village sold all kinds of things, both groceries and hardware – pots and pans, coal scuttles, buckets, cigarettes, pipe tobacco, twist cut off the block to be smoked in the pipe or for the miners to use as chewing tobacco, rabbit food, hen corn, firewood sticks and so on. All the food came to the shops in either sacks or barrels, and had to be weighed up on the premises.

Clothes were also very scarce in the 1940s and the only time you got new ones, if you were lucky, was for the Whitsuntide weekend. They were mainly from the Co-operative drapery in the next village and on the tick, being paid for weekly over the rest of the year.'

A pony and trap used as transport for an outing in 1943. It was once also the family business – milk was delivered to the doorstep with a churn and ladled into jugs covered by bead-edged muslin cloths.

'In pre-supermarket days, Pudsey had Althams, the Maypole, the Co-op (several departments) and two privately owned grocers in the town centre – JC Booth and Galloways. I remember biscuits weighed out loose from glass-lidded tins, dry goods weighed out into blue or brown bags, returning jam jars to the Maypole (if I remember correctly, it was a penny for a two pound jar and a halfpenny for a one pound jar), and standing watching, fascinated, as butter was cut and patted into shape with a pattern on top!'

'Before the war the edges of Ossett town were mostly rural and, besides their farms, local families such as the Nettletons, Etheringtons, Welburns and Harrisons ran businesses such as milk rounds, delivered fresh from the cows by horse and cart twice a day. A few ran butchers' shops, killing their own livestock, and they also supplied fresh eggs.

Besides Ossett's own market, the surrounding area was well

This Ford van was used by another family firm for their milk deliveries from 1933 onwards.

blessed with markets. Dewsbury, Batley and Wakefield were all very distinctive with cheap food, clothing and local characters. Dewsbury was usually visited twice a week by many housewives, to buy fish and, on Saturday, as a special treat cakes from either Dempster Listers or Credwells cake shop. We never bought bread because that was made at home. I can smell the lovely oven bottom cakes today, eaten while still warm with either butter or dripping spread on them.'

'In the 1960s I moved from Lancashire to live in Horsforth. Shopping for certain things was a bit of a puzzle to me at first, when I had to go to the butcher's for tripe and the confectioner's for pork pies, whereas I had always bought both these items at a fish and chip shop in Lancashire – where the pies were mostly beef and if I wanted a pork pie I went to the pork butcher's!'

'Going back to the 1930s, I remember Birdsedge village had a post office, secondhand furniture store and another shop and drapery which also sold corn for farmers. The local Co-op was at Shepley and a man walked round for the orders on Wednesday, deliveries were on Thursday with the butchery on Friday. "Divi" day was a highlight twice a year when the Co-op paid its dividend and was very important in poor households. I remember my mother and aunt walking through the snow to collect it, at 3s 3d in the pound it was well worth it. There was also a local butcher came round and the paraffin man who sold paraffin, polishes, soaps etc and also sweets including red and black liquorice bootlaces which we thought were wonderful even though they tasted of paraffin. Ice cream was also delivered made from milk at local farms. We had a fish and chip shop in the village, above the Crown, opened by my uncle. My grandmother soaked the ham bone (for the peas) at home and made the batter, then carried it to the shop in white enamel buckets. The local pub bought the salt in the hope that customers would use too much and need to quench their thirst next door in the pub.'

STREET TRADERS

*B*esides the delivery men, the streets were busy with men and women selling everything from hot peas to kippers!

⊠ STREET LIFE IN A MINING VILLAGE IN THE 1920S ⊠

'From the houses to the village shops and the colliery was about a mile. With no form of transport, street vendors were an essential part of village life. They were very regular in their habits. You could almost tell the time by them.

Known as the knocker-up, the man with the long pole would come as early as 4.30 in the morning to wake the miners. Every male over the age of 14 worked at the colliery. The knocker-up would be paid sixpence a week to wake whoever lived in the house by stretching out his long pole and banging the end of it on the bedroom window. He would keep banging until he got an answer which meant that someone in the house had to get out of bed before he was satisfied they were awake and he could go on to the next house on his list.

Milk was delivered daily by a local farmer in a milk float pulled by a white horse. He was easily recognised by the clopping sound of the horse's hooves on the road and the farmer's familiar, "Whoah" as he steered the horse to a halt. The horse knew every stop on the route. As the farmer came out of one gate and went to the next house, the horse moved along with him and stopped at each gate and waited until the milkman came out, then moved on again, all the way along the street. The milk was served into your jug from metal gill and pint measures from a large churn.

The short fat middle-aged man with a handlebar moustache arrived twice a week to sell pikelets, often referred to as muffins today. He carried a large basket over his arm and his goods were covered by a sparkling white tea towel. You could hear his handbell ringing as he called out, "Any yeast," for he sold fresh yeast too. Most housewives baked their own bread at least twice a week and relied on him to deliver their yeast regularly.

If you were short of bread, a widow who lived in the street would sell you one of the home-baked loaves she baked nearly every day.

Another old lady made delicious cream toffee and supplemented it with sweets she bought from a shop in the village. Every Saturday morning, as soon as they were given their weekly pocket money of a penny or a halfpenny, children in the street would take it to Mrs Linstead. Eyes bulging at the assortment of jelly babies, chocolate eclairs, pear drops, liquorice sticks, torpedoes, coconut mushrooms, treacle toffee and chocolate bars laid out on her kitchen table, they would spend as long as possible choosing what to buy until the old lady began to get impatient. The kitchen had a sickly sweet smell of its own. When you were young it seemed like heaven.

Two elderly sisters sold pop, in the old-style bottles with a marble in the top. To buy lemonade, Tizer or dandelion and burdock was a great treat on a Sunday afternoon, especially in the summer. If you had an empty bottle to take back the pop would only cost threepence instead of four. Getting a penny back on the bottle was part of the fun.

Ice cream first came in the form of a hard brick which you were given together with two thin wafers; you put them together to make up a sandwich. The man would yell out in a high pitched, falsetto voice, "Who likes hokey pokey?" and "hokey pokey, penny a lump." In a few minutes the street would be full of young folks who, if they hadn't already tried it were ready to have a go.

The mussel man called every Friday. He had a flat cart with a huge pile of fresh mussels on it. When you heard the shout, "Any mussels," you ran to get a large basin in case he set off before you got to the cart and you had to go running after him. He scooped the mussels off the cart into a large heavy quart measure, for they were only sold by the quart. First you washed the mussels then put them into a large pan and covered them with water and put them to boil over the fire. If you let them boil over, the water came over the top of the pan and very nearly put the fire out.

For years the greengrocer, who had a shop in the village, came every Tuesday and Friday with his horse and a large flat cart with a tarpaulin that he pulled over to cover the fruit if it was raining. When he got too old his son came instead.

He fell in love with the Silver Prize Band conductor's daughter and would stop for hours at her house, leaving the horse to paw the ground outside. Housewives wanting to prepare potatoes for dinner took a dim view of this and would send their children to find him. It made no difference when they did find him for he wouldn't leave the house to serve them. Young boys had a great time, sneaking up behind the cart when they thought no one was looking, grabbing an orange or an apple, running around the other side and across the nearest garden and out of sight.

When the rag man came, shouting at the top of his voice, "Any rags," or "Any empty jam jars," the children would run in the house yelling, pestering for rags. For only a few rags or a small one pound jam jar, you could get a goldfish or a balloon. With more rags or a bigger, two pound jar, the goldfish would be in a bowl.

Sometimes an old lorry came, rattling all the way from the pots, pans, brown kettles and shiny metal teapots hanging from its sides. The man sold teapot strainers and pan and kettle menders by the dozen. He would sit inside the cab, honking on a big fat horn, waiting until people came out to the lorry.

A familiar sight was a ton of coal tipped beside a gate. Miners were allowed one free ton of coal a month as part of their wages. Sometimes there would be as many as eight tons tipped on the same day. In the winter, there would be a frantic ringing and scraping of shovels as people made a great effort to get the coal into the coalhouse before dark.

On Sunday mornings the Salvation Army arrived to sing their hymns of praise at two or three stops along the street. Carols were played on Christmas morning by the Silver Prize Band, sponsored by the colliery owners. They stopped at each street corner and could be heard all over the estate. At the end of a carol, miners would come out with bottles of beer or invite bandsmen into their homes to slake their thirst until they

Bob Lofthouse, milkman in the Stanbury area in the early 1900s.

reached the next corner. It really was a Merry Christmas.'

▨ YEAST, KIPPERS AND PEAS! ▨

'On Monday tea-times at Dewsbury a man came round selling kippers and bananas. My grandma always had a kipper, but we could choose one or the other. It was an odd combination!

Every few weeks the scissor and knife grinder came round. He pedalled with his foot to make a wheel of emery go round, and sparks used to fly in all directions.

The pack man called with a big suitcase. He sold clothes, wool, elastic, buttons and pins and needles along with drapery, towels, sheets and pillowcases, table covers and tea towels. If the items were very costly people paid so much a week. On Wednesdays a lady came round selling fresh yeast ready for baking day on Thursday, and another character was "Ruddle Rhoda" who herself quarried the soft sandstone and walked for miles around the district selling it. A few evenings a week a man came round selling peas. These were small grey-brown peas in a liquid we called gravy. His container was like a dustbin mounted on a hand cart with a coal fire underneath to keep the peas hot. He used to shout, "Peas are hot, penny a pot", and we would take out our own pot or basin and get it filled for a penny. We added salt, pepper and vinegar and ate them with a spoon.

The rag-and-bone man came round the streets with a horse and cart, collecting rags and metal. Sometimes when we left school at lunch-time he would give us a leaflet, and if we took him our old rags on our way back to school in the afternoon he would give us a goldfish in a jam jar, or other small gift. If our mothers gave him the rags they would get a few pennies, which helped the family budget, especially if it was the back end of the week and they were waiting for the wages, which were paid in cash every Friday.'

'The yeast man at Armley had beautiful brass scales and he would break the yeast out of its muslin wrapping and sell it on the doorstep.'

'The favourite with the children, of course, was the ice cream man. In the 1930s in Leeds one rode his bicycle with a box on the front in which he kept the ice-cream. "Stop Me and Buy One" was his cry. Another ice cream man was the "Hokey Pokey" man.

As children we were generally wary of gypsies, having been told many a tale of them stealing anything from clothes on the washing line to babies from their prams! The gypsies sold pegs and told fortunes and always had ways of wheedling money from people or they cursed non-givers. Shirley remembers her mother being conned into buying bulbs. "Dancing Princesses," promised the gypsy woman, with her basket on her arm and her baby strapped to her back. The gypsies may have called the bulbs "Dancing Princesses," but we called them bluebells when they came up!

Another popular character on the streets was the "Tingle Lairy" man; he trundled his street organ from street to street playing for pennies whilst the children danced in the road and often encouraged their young mothers to dance too.

In the afternoon the tea-cake seller carried his tray round the streets calling "Brown-cakes, tea-cakes, lovely ½d buns". Then as evening fell, the lamplighter carrying his ladder walked the streets that still had gas lighting.

The rag and bone man made frequent visits, giving balloons to children who brought out old clothes. The ammonia man called "Mony-mony-aye" to advertise the ammonia he sold to go in the washing and the donkey stone man would often follow him selling stones that would whiten door steps. Houseproud housewives would clean even the outside steps and many would whiten the edges just so they would not be "shown up" by their neighbours.'

FROM THE CRADLE TO THE GRAVE

We were far more likely to be born, to suffer our illnesses and to die in our own homes in the past. Many families, before the NHS, relied on tried and trusted home remedies rather than call out the doctor, who had to be paid. There were some illnesses, though, that meant a stay in an isolation hospital, including those scourges of childhood – scarlet fever and diphtheria.

▨ HOME CURES ▨

'Home remedies abounded. A sore throat was treated with a salt water gargle, or egg yolks beaten into sugar. Splinters in fingers were dealt with by making a paste of sugar and soap and putting this mixture on a bandage, as a poultice, overnight. The splinter was usually either out altogether or easily withdrawn the next day.'

'Elderberries were made into syrup, and raspberries into a vinegar, both of which were very good for a cold. If you had a goose you saved all the fat and rubbed it on for a bad chest. It

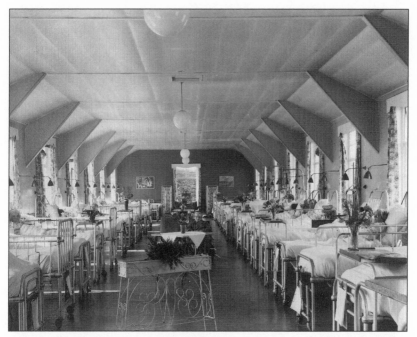

'A' ward at St John's Hospital, Keighley in 1961 – originally built for wounded soldiers in the First World War.

would smell terrible but seemed to do the trick. A doctor or a chemist was a last resort.'

'When the Irish navvies came to resurface the main road with their steam rollers and burning machines, all the children in the area around Roberttown were sent to stand over the braziers which had pots of melting tar to fill in the gaps in the road. This was to clear our chests and keep us free from colds in the winter.'

'Castor oil and prune paste were given for constipation. For a sore throat my mother used to put sulphur on a piece of newspaper and with my mouth open wide, she would blow the sulphur down my throat. Camphorated oil was rubbed on my chest and then a piece of flannel pinned to my vest to keep me warm. Also a piece of flannel about 1½ inches wide was tied round my neck for a sore throat and I had to go to school with it on and I was frightened if anyone should see it. If we had a temperature, we were given yarrow tea, and for a stomach upset, it was camomile flowers scalded in a jug and we had to drink it. That was awful. For a bad chest, it was kaolin poultice. That was spread hot on a cloth and fastened to the vest on the chest. If my mouth was sore with ulcers, etc my mother would mix honey with borax and rub it on my gums. I thought that was very nice.'

'Although the present National Health Service is not all one would wish for, the times before it came into being were hard for those who could not afford to pay for a doctor's services. As a result, many old herbal remedies and family recipes passed down from generation to generation were used to cure various illnesses. Children were dosed with Virol and Scott's Emulsion (both of which I loved) to prevent colds. Squares of camphor encased in a little flannel bag were pinned to undergarments to ward off infections.

An onion was sliced and then sprinkled with demerara sugar, was allowed to stand and the resulting liquor drained off and taken three times a day. I still use this today and it works for a dry cough. Staying with onions, my Gran always used to rub a wasp sting with the cut side of an onion to take away the pain and irritation.

Another cough medicine was made with a pennyworth each of olive oil, ipecacuanha wine, oil of almonds, syrup of violets, and syrup of squills. Put all into a bottle and shake well, take one teaspoonful three times a day. My mother used to make this for the family's coughs in the 1930s.

My mother's favourite home made cough medicine in the 1940s was equal quantities of butter, black treacle and vinegar mixed together in a basin and kept warm and liquid on top of the oven in the Yorkist range.

To ease the pain of earache me Mam always kept one of me Dad's old wool socks full of salt in the oven by the fire, this was applied to the affected ear and the warmth always helped ease the pain.

If ever we were lucky enough to have a goose for Christmas my mother always kept the fat in stone jars to rub on chests and backs for chesty colds.

I can remember going to the local chemist in Holbeck in the late 1940s every Saturday morning for a "worm cake", this was like a large chocolate drop with coloured hundreds and thousands on top. For tummy aches Mam always bought a bottle of Nurse Harvey's Mixture. I remember once drinking a whole bottle full because I loved it, and filling the bottle with water so my Mam wouldn't know. She did, of course, mothers always seemed to know everything. For colds and fevers Mam always bought us Scissors Powders, these came in little folds of paper and had a picture of a pair of scissors on the front. To relieve a chesty cough we always asked the chemist to make us up a bottle of *"Drops off the Shelf"*. I don't know how it got its name but it was nice, sort of liquorice, and it warmed a sore chest.'

'In springtime in the 1930s we used to go into the fields around Dewsbury to collect young nettles, about two carriers full, and my grandmother would boil them and drink the water "to clear the blood". Sometimes she added them to a stew.

At that time you paid the doctor so much a week all year round, which a man collected for him, and when you were ill you just hoped there was enough money to your credit to cover the cost. The dentist used to come to your house. I remember him pulling mother's teeth out. She sat in a chair facing the window with a bucket of water beside her into which the dentist dropped each tooth, and into which she could spit when she rinsed her mouth out. We children sat in the same room and watched the whole episode!'

❖ NEWLY ARRIVED ❖

'There is a short service in the Book of Common Prayer for the Churching of Women as a thanksgiving after childbirth. I was "churched" after each of my children were born in the 1950s. A friend of mine said her grandmother wouldn't let her in the house until she'd been churched, as till then you were considered to be "unclean". This seemed to be a common superstition in the area where I was living.'

'I was born in March 1947. My parents, who lived in Grimsby at the time were on holiday in Leeds, staying with my maternal grandparents who lived in Holbeck.

I wasn't due until the middle of April but my Mum started with backache and the local midwife said she thought the baby needed turning and so she told Mum to go to the local maternity hospital for a check. It was knee deep in snow and there were no trams, buses or taxis running, so Mum and Dad had to walk the four miles from Holbeck to Hyde Terrace Hospital.

Mum felt hungry on the way so thinking there was no rush to get there as I wasn't due for another month they bought fish and chips to eat on the way.

They finally arrived at the hospital and I was born on the trolley in the hospital corridor, weighing four pounds and a month premature. The doctor and midwife told my Mum and Dad they would never rear me as I was so tiny and eight month babies rarely survived. Needless to say, I did survive; the hospital charged my Dad £6 17s for my delivery and my Mum's one week stay at the hospital after my birth.'

▓ CHILDISH AILMENTS ▓

'The so-called childish ailments which afflicted children in the 1920s and 1930s could be quite serious. Measles could leave a child with deafness or bad eyesight. The recommended practice was to lie in bed with the curtains drawn and certainly no books allowed. We had a super doctor and he painted red spots on my sister's doll. Another of his tricks was to sit us on his knee then tell us to say "aah" at the same time opening his legs so that we fell on the floor. I don't know whether he charged extra for this privilege; maybe not since he was married to Mummy's cousin. I think the usual fee was 5s a visit; one tried to call him out as seldom as possible.

If you were unlucky enough to catch scarlet fever or diphtheria you were taken to the isolation hospital and all the things you had been using were burnt, often your favourite toy

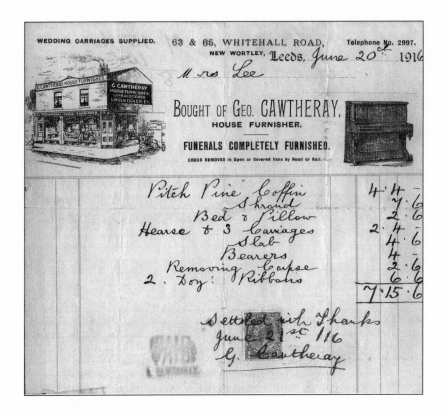

The receipt reads:

WEDDING CARRIAGES SUPPLIED.   63 & 65, WHITEHALL ROAD,   Telephone No. 2997.
NEW WORTLEY, Leeds, June 20th 1916

Mrs Lee

BOUGHT OF GEO. CAWTHERAY,
HOUSE FURNISHER.

FUNERALS COMPLETELY FURNISHED.

GOODS REMOVED in Open or Covered Vans by Road or Rail.

	£	s	d
Pitch Pine Coffin	4	4	–
Shroud		7	6
Bed & Pillow		2	6
Hearse & 3 Carriages	2	4	–
Slab		4	6
Bearers		4	–
Removing Corpse		2	6
2. Doy: Ribbons		6	6
	7	15	6

Settled with Thanks
June 21st /16
G. Cawtheray

Cawtheray's of Leeds also arranged funerals.

or book. My sister and I were lucky and never had either disease. The progress of the children in hospital was put on a daily bulletin board at the council offices on the green (now the museum). Each child was given a number and one looked to see if the patient was "satisfactory", "poorly", "critical" or even dead; such was the seriousness of the diseases before inoculation eradicated them.'

'I was unwell with a bad throat and the doctor was summoned. Within an hour I was being wrapped in a bright red blanket and carried to a waiting ambulance, which took me to the local fever hospital. There, with diphtheria, I spent the next seven weeks. I remember lying flat on my back for the first week and then I was allowed to sit up. I don't remember much about the food except supper, which was always cold rice pudding served in an earthenware mug. The nurses were very kind and attentive, and the ward was kept spotless. Every morning a cleaning lady polished the floor. Parents could visit at weekends only and had to stay outside in the open. Patients' beds were pushed up to a window, and conversation had to be shouted through the glass. As it was winter my Mum and Dad must have been extremely cold. When I was finally allowed out of bed my legs were so wobbly, it was like learning to walk again. I had a further three weeks at home before being allowed back to school. The fever hospital is no longer needed thanks to immunisation, and closed some years ago.'

▣ A FUNERAL IN THE VILLAGE ▣

'We always knew when there was going to be a funeral in the village as we would see the farmer leading his two well-groomed black horses up the field. He had collected them from a neighbouring farm where they were kept. In a little while, the farmer, a sharp featured individual, wearing a long black coat, shiny top hat and sombre expression to match the occasion, would drive the two beplumed horses down the hill. They would be pulling the ornamental hearse.

As I look back, it always seemed to be raining when I saw the black horses come down the field. The road to the cemetery was very steep and many a time they would have difficulty in dragging the heavy hearse up to the top.'

CHILDHOOD & SCHOOLDAYS

CHILDHOOD DAYS

We grew up with a degree of freedom and security sadly unknown to many of today's children – is it any wonder that we remember long hot summer days and the fun of cold snowy winters! As we grew older there were new delights to be experienced.

❖ MEMORIES OF A MINER'S CHILD ❖

'When I was a child, the two-minutes' silence was always observed on 11th November, no matter on which day of the week it occurred. The school I attended was opposite the local branch of the Co-op. The windows of my classroom overlooked the street. As eleven o'clock approached, the class stood behind their desks, waiting for the pit buzzer to blow, signalling the silence. At that moment, the doors of the Co-op opened and out stepped a large lady, holding in front of her a large, unwrapped, white chamber pot, decorated with pink roses. She stood rigidly to attention until the buzzer announced the end of the silence and, looking neither right nor left made her way down the street towards that part of the village where, I knew, the houses had no indoor toilets. I can picture the incident still. As an impressionable 13 year old, I had a struggle to control my amusement and very nearly forgot the reason I was standing behind my chair.

The annual children's outing to the seaside was a day looked forward to by all the miners' children in the village where I lived as a child. All year my father would buy raffle tickets from the Miners' Institute and the Working Men's Club.

Everyone would be up before five o'clock in the morning on the day. There would be such excitement and it was always a scramble to make sure you had remembered everything and would be ready on time. Sometimes, as many as 15 buses would

Irene and Joyce in the height of fashion in the 1930s. Most children got new 'best' clothes only at Whitsuntide.

leave the village in convoy, travelling to Bridlington, Cleethorpes, Scarborough and once to Morecambe.

At what was always called the Halfway House, though it usually seemed further than halfway to me, the buses stopped and all the children were shepherded into a long hall, where we sat on benches at trestle tables, covered sparsely with white paper tablecloths. Then we were given a dish of cornflakes, a potted meat sandwich and an apple which you could eat later on the bus. There wasn't enough time to eat it at the table as you had to join a long queue for the few, not very clean toilets and rush back to the bus.

When we went to Morecambe, my younger sister fell in the sea wearing all her clothes. Mother was frantic and afraid she would catch cold as the weather wasn't too warm. She left me on the beach to look after my younger brother, telling me not to move. Off she went, taking my sister with her, to buy new clothes. I had never been left on my own before and of course, Father was nowhere to be seen. He had gone off to the pub with his cronies. After what seemed like hours but was probably only ten minutes, I left the beach and began walking up and down the promenade looking for my mother. When I did eventually find her, she was with a policeman. She was so upset. All I got was a clip around the ear for not doing as I was told.

Before the opening of pit head baths, the miners came home in their pit clothes. I can recall the day my father arrived home, calling out to my mother to shut the back door before he would come into the house. The waistcoat he was wearing had large pockets in which he would carry his snap tin and water bottle, known as a dudley.

Mother and I watched from the window as he stood in the garden and took off his waistcoat, shaking it vigorously as he did so. From the pockets, mice flew in all directions. Although my father made an energetic effort and lashed out with the waistcoat, he didn't succeed in catching any of them. He had felt the movement as he walked up the street but did nothing about it until he was in a position to take off his waistcoat.

Behind our house was what I called the buttercup field. In the summer I would climb over the fence and lie on my back in the field, letting my imagination run riot as I watched the white clouds changing shape, fires, faces, monsters and angels. Several wild flowers grew in the field, daisies, buttercups, clover, a few wild oats and barley.

At the top of the field was a farm where I would sometimes be sent for fresh milk if we ran short. I would take the blue enamel can with the fitted lid and go up the hill, through the wide green door of the farmhouse. When I knocked on the window, the farmer's wife would come into the scrubbed stone-flagged scullery, lift the window and serve the milk from a large churn. The only other thing in that cold-looking room was a huge white-wood table.

I loved to hear the colliery band practising. On summer evenings, they would play in the Miners' Institute. When the windows were open, the sound would drift up to where I lived. As a special treat, I would be allowed to go down the field and sit on a low wall outside the band room for half an hour. The band is still one of the leading silver bands in the country and I follow its fortunes with deep interest.

Both my parents were competent musicians and Sunday evenings, especially during the winter, were usually spent around the piano. After tea, Uncle Harold would come and, accompanied by my mother on the piano, would sing, in his thin tenor voice, the drawing room ballads of the day, such as *The Last Rose of Summer* and *Danny Boy*.

Mother was a trained singer and had a rich, mezzo-soprano voice. She was especially pleased when, one year, she was asked to sing at the miners' annual Christmas dinner, which she and my father always attended, as my father was an overman at the pit. For weeks, Dad's cousin Winnie came on Monday mornings and played whilst my mother got her voice tuned to perfection in time for the big event. She sang *The Lost Chord* and *Alice Blue Gown* on that occasion. It was a very special night out for her and she had many compliments on her singing, from the pit officials and their wives. I often wondered how she coped with the black taffeta dress she wore, for the skirt was covered in gold and silver sequins which made it very heavy.

Mother looked forward to Sunday morning when the *Empire*

News was delivered. She would turn to the page where there was a half page of Tin Pan Alley style sheet music, then dash into the front room to try it out on the piano. *Connie in the Cornfield* and *Horsey, Keep Your Tail Up*, are only two titles I remember. In the evening she would do the competitions and every week bought *Tit-Bits* and *John Bull*, to help her with slogans that were asked for. She won several small prizes, among them a fountain pen and a breakfast set.

Since he was a boy, my father had played a concertina. When he grew up, he still played and would stand with his back to the fire, legs astride and for his party piece would play *The Bluebells of Scotland*. When he got to the end he would play up and down the scale, like a peal of bells, swinging the concertina in a circle, around and above his head. It was very sweet and very real; sounded just like a peal of bells.

There was great excitement in the house when our first wireless arrived. It was a very ugly piece of grey metal with three open sides, an open top and three valves. I watched through the window as workmen dug a hole at the bottom of the back garden and proceeded to erect a tall, black tarred pole, with a wire attached to it running to the house. For a long time, it could only be heard through earphones which my parents took it in turn to use. As it was the first one in the street, all the neighbours were invited in to listen.

When I was older, I had to take a battery to be charged once a week to a shop near the school. The man in the shop was an awful gossip and being a shy child, I was afraid to interrupt him with the result I was always late for school. On the way home I would collect the newly charged battery so that we could hear the wireless that night. If I forgot, I would be sent back for it. Once, acid from the battery spilled on my coat and burnt a large hole in it. That was a catastrophe.'

▒ LONG HOT SUMMER DAYS ▒

'I lived in a big old rambling house situated at the corner of a four acre field with a smallholding attached. We used to go running across the meadow holding on to each other's dress pretending to be a train and the boy in front was the engine. We went through a gate at the bottom of the meadow and scrambled down to a lovely sandy bay with the river flowing by; we pretended to be at Brighton on our holidays, and we played all morning in the clean golden sand where we were sheltered from the winds, but we knew not to go too near the river's edge.

There were four of us who had to walk a mile each day to the nearest Church of England school. The school was built at the top of a steep slope; at the bottom of this steep bending path were some old fashioned tipple toilets which flushed themselves every so often. When there was snow and frost on the ground we had to use an old bucket in the spare classroom which was half full of broken chairs.

At Christmas we had a faith tea, and each child was asked to bring something, buns, jellies, sandwiches etc. One of us would ask the dirty girl, whose hair was full of jaspers, now called lice, what she had brought. She would say buttered currant teacake, so we told each other not to eat any currant teacake.

At lunchtime we had to walk out on to the main road and down a slope to one of the cottages to have our pot of tea or cocoa mashed, for which we paid one halfpenny. If she gave the contents also it cost us one penny. If it was windy our pot of cocoa was nearly cold, at least what was left after we had spilt some.

Sometimes on a hot sunny day in August we would go after lunch to the churchyard at the top of the hill and each asked for a piece of rag to wipe our noses on. As we went through the gate we said no laughing or singing songs, we are in God's garden. We would go to the old part and choose two neglected gravestones and we each got a jar from the rubbish heap, and filled it with water to wash the gravestones using the rags. After, we dug and pulled the grass and weeds away, always taking care not to let anyone see us as we knew they would not believe we were doing a good turn and would send us away. To finish our good deed we collected all the good flowers from several discarded bunches plus some leaves and ferns and placed them in the jam jars of clean water on the cleaned up graves, which could be up to 100 years old. If after rubbing for several minutes some gold lettering appeared, we thought we had performed a miracle.'

'In the late 1940s we used to go to Kirkby Overblow in the summer. Mum would pack a picnic and we would go on a tram into Leeds and then catch a bus out, walking across two fields to the river. There was a donkey in one of the fields and we always took him a carrot. When we reached the river Dad would blow up the lorry or tractor tyre inner tubes, and we would put on our swimming costumes and play in the river. A lady in one of the cottages nearby sold pots of tea and home-made cakes and ice cream. The summer days always seemed long and hot then.'

▦ THE LAMPLIGHTER ▦

'It was dark when I awoke, but as my eyes grew accustomed to the darkness I knew that this was going to be a very special day. I was eight years old, in October 1926, and my greatest wish was to be given to me for my present. This was what I had begged and pleaded for, and only the promise of "when you are eight" quietened me.

After breakfast I went off to school but didn't concentrate very much on my lessons and at four o'clock I didn't wait for my friends but ran home to get ready for my adventure. My mother brought my thick woolly cardigan and as it was October and very chilly, an extra pair of socks. On the stroke of 4.30 pm there was a knock at the door and when I opened it my eyes shone. He was very tall and thin and looked quite old but I put out my hand and as he grasped it, I was the proudest child in the village.

He was the lamplighter and I had been chosen to go with him on his journey round the village. The long wooden pole was placed over his left shoulder and we started off. When we reached the first lamp I stood and watched as the small glass bulb at the end of the pole was pushed inside the gas lamp. Suddenly there was a pop and the gas mantle burst into light. At the second lamp I was allowed to help hold the wooden pole and this was my very special present.

After walking up and down several streets I eventually

arrived back home, tired and hungry, but knowing that I had never enjoyed a present so much.'

◪ SUMMER AND WINTER ◪

'Our family of four girls and two boys lived on the outskirts of a mining village at Purston, and I well remember the lovely plantation across the main road into which we would go after school to find tadpoles and little frogs. Mum never worried about us and we used to roam miles just taking a bottle of water. Down the country lanes we skipped and jumped gathering bluebells or wild roses in the woods or milkmaids, cowslips and daisies in Shelton's field a little bit higher up the road from where we lived. Happy, carefree days! We also pulled petals off while counting "love me, love me not". There was hardly anyone about and no traffic at all. Fancy skipping with one pal at one side of the main road and another at the other side, holding a long straw-plaited rope which we got from the greengrocer's. These ropes had been wrapped round crates of bananas from abroad. If we heard the clippety-clop, clippety-clop of a horse we just waited, put the rope down while he passed, then set off again, sometimes when we were on our way to school. I was seven to eight years old in 1919.

On winter nights, how we liked to stand in the bay window and watch the lamplighter come up the road with his long pole lighting the gas lamps! Then it was upstairs to bed, one of us carrying a candle in a bright red enamel candle stick. "Be careful," Mum would say, "I don't want any candle grease on the carpet." We would kneel down by the bed my sister and I shared to say our prayers – "Gentle Jesus" – and hop into bed. "No talking mind," Mum would shout. We carefully blew the candle out but as the wick changed from red to black it smelt awful, so we would wet our thumb and forefinger with our tongue and nip the candle out. We took it in turns. When a real gale was blowing we could hear the very big trees in the plantation across the road making a big noise just like a rough sea.

We were lucky children really because after Dad came home, we used to go to the seaside at Bridlington for a week's holiday a year; but some of our school pals never saw the sea in those days. Two brothers we knew had to share their boots: Tommy's turn one week and James had them the next. Many children's jumpers had great holes in the elbows, and one little girl was literally fastened up in safety pins, boots and all. If we had toothache we sure had toothache! No aspirins or painkillers at all! Life was rather tough in many ways, but at least we were not afraid of being molested. People were poorer then but very honest. No one locked the door during the day and some never locked it at night. When we were in our teens mother always insisted we were in by ten o'clock. "No respectable person is out after that," she used to say. True enough, the streets were deserted except for the local "bobby" with his shoulder cape on.'

▣ HOLIDAYS WITH GRANDPARENTS ▣

'My grandparents lived in a large house and country estate on the outskirts of Leeds. We as children spent all our holidays there, in the 1930s.

My grandfather was of the Victorian era, very strict and where children were definitely seen and not heard. My grandmother used to take 13 to 14 year old young girls from the orphanage and train them into housemaids. They came pale, thin and miserable and left as healthy young ladies with a job to go to.

Meal times were very strict, everyone had to be properly dressed and if you were late you missed that course. As children we always had to have ground rice before a jelly. Sunday lunch was very special. I would help Grandmother to polish all the fruit, nuts etc and display it in beautiful silver dishes on a side table. The meal always started with turbot, followed by roast beef, sweets for the children, cheese and biscuits, dessert and then port for the gentlemen.

We attended church three times on Sundays. At Christmas there was a huge tree covered with lighted candles (a real fire hazard) and on Christmas Eve the hand-bell ringers used to come and perform in the house.'

'We had no television in the 1930s but enjoyed listening to the wireless. Living at New Mill, Huddersfield, we went to dances held at local schools and wore long dresses and silver shoes and used Tangee lipstick and *Evening in Paris* perfume hoping the local lads would ask us to dance the waltz, quickstep and sometimes, greatly daring, the tango. We had an annual choir dance where we danced the Lancers and were often swung off our feet in the final set by over-enthusiastic partners.

Saturdays were spent playing tennis in summer and we had American tournaments and picnic teas on the tennis courts at New Mill Institute. Then we would go dancing or to the pictures at night. We had a cinema in Holmfirth two miles away and we would meet our boyfriends on the bridge outside the cinema and go to the second house on Saturdays and then walk home, sometimes eating fish and chips. We had two open air swimming pools in Holmfirth – the Lido and the Ash Grove which was bigger and had more room to sunbathe after we had been swimming.

Easter always seemed to be hot and sunny and out would come our shorts and cameras and we would go hiking round the Wessenden Valley and then catch a trolley bus at Marsden and go to the pictures or the Easter Fair in Huddersfield.

Holidays were taken in August (usually in the second week) and all the local mills shut down for a week and some of the shops shut. People flocked to the seaside to Blackpool, Scarborough, Morecambe and then "down south" to Bournemouth and Torquay as more people got motor cars.

We took part in an open-air version of *Merrie England* and I was a dancing girl, but the weather was unkind in July 1939 and it was decided to stage it again in September but on 3rd September we were at war with Germany and that was the end of that. Boys we knew went to war and some never came back. In 1943 I was called up for service in the ATS and it was October 1946 before I went back to live in New Mill. Life was never the same again.'

◙ GREAT MEMORIES ◙

'The year was 1951 – Festival of Britain year. I came home from school one day to find that my dancing class teacher had called to ask me if I would be a mannequin in a fashion show to be held in Slaithwaite as part of the local celebrations.

I was 13 at the time and so thrilled because it was my ambition of the moment to be a mannequin, which was the name given to models in those days. I went along to Heywoods Fashion Store in Huddersfield to try on the clothes I would wear in the show. I was given dresses, coats, nightwear, and a lovely party dress.

The great day came at last. There were eight children and 14 adults. I was so excited and although I was used to being in dancing class concerts I was very nervous. We did the fashion shows for three days and had a wonderful time.

Days later we were asked to Heywoods for a tea party and we were presented with Festival of Britain Crown coins by the Colne Valley Urban District Council and also asked to choose one of the items we had worn in the show. My choice was one of the lovely coats. I enjoyed myself immensely and have great memories of September 1951.'

◙ THE CONTINENTAL COFFEE BAR ◙

'My first experience of the Continental coffee bar was on a sunny Saturday lunchtime with my worldly, confident 16 year old sister. We met up with a group of her friends for a chat over a bottle of Coke. I felt awkward, a stranger, who at 13 was too young to belong to this sophisticated place. In reality it was no more than a huge cellar beneath a busy Bradford street, where all the town's youth with Mod tendencies congregated, no doubt every town had such a place in the mid 1960s.

Within months of that first visit, I felt thoroughly at home there with my fourth year school friends, meeting regularly for a chat and of course, to meet boys. Boys in green parkas with short haircuts, arriving in a buzz of scooters, the number of which never amounted to the number of crash helmets, possessively clutched under arms like carefully nurtured dinosaur eggs.

As nonchalantly as possible you had to negotiate a steep flight

At the 1951 Festival of Britain fashion show in Heywoods Fashion Store, Huddersfield.

of open-sided stairs into the centre of the room, knowing that your feet and legs, all of them, considering the fashion at the time, were in full view long before you had any idea who was there to see them. Descending into a dark red glow of friendship and familiarity, first to brave the cold welcome of the gloomy middle-aged Greek, exchanging a handful of coins for a bottle of Coke, which he knew would last you the whole evening. The almost casual turn, taking in every face in a second. The ex-boyfriend, the limpet-like girl hanging on his arm, neither of whom you will ever speak to again. Huddles of familiar strangers in their own circles around formica tables, and finally, to your own territory in the far corner, praying that someone is there already, to smile and wave, just to outwardly show you belong.

Usually everyone had arrived by seven o'clock and as the evening progressed it grew louder and hotter. The juke box blared the latest hits, the football table clattered, and girls chattered of fashions, their latest acquisitions from Top Girl or Valances, comforting broken hearts, encouraging flirtations, or just planning the next night at the Mecca. Every single square foot was occupied with the exception of the quiet pool of light surrounding the Greek and his counter. The dreaded home time loomed as always, the last minute lingering before the dash up the stairs and 100 yard sprint for the nine o'clock bus.

For more than two years I happily whiled away my teens in that cellar, going through all the agonies of falling in and out of love on an almost weekly basis, spots, puppy-fat and uncertainties, but they were all shared agonies and never since then have I felt the comfortable closeness of such friends as these.

Finally, one sunny Saturday lunchtime, a worldly confident 16 year old, I met up with a couple of friends for a chat over a bottle of Coke in the Continental, and glanced around. I felt awkward, a stranger too sophisticated for this dark red cellar full of kids. I walked up the stairs, out into the sunshine.'

GAMES AND TREATS

Spending the Saturday penny was always a serious business!
Our games came round in their seasons and we played most of
them out in the street, with little traffic to worry us.

▣ THE HIGHLIGHT OF MY WEEK ▣

'Saturday was the highlight of my week, when I would take
my Saturday penny and visit the local sweetshop. I couldn't
afford chocolates at 4d for a quarter, but toffees were 2d a quarter
so I could get two ounces if I wanted. My favourites were
cheaper still and I could get four different sorts for a farthing an
ounce.

Apart from the Saturday penny we had no money for sweets,
except for the odd halfpenny cornet in summer when the ice
cream cart came round, but we would beg a spoonful of sugar
mixed with a bit of cocoa from our mothers and dip a finger in it
to suck. Most mothers kept a stick of hard black liquorice, bought
at the chemist's as medication. From a chip of this we would
make a bottle full of "Spanish juice" to drink.'

'During the early 1930s in Batley, around Shrove Tuesday one of
the local confectioners used to come out in the street and empty
out the few remaining sweets in each jar. I was one of the eager
children waiting for this magic moment.'

▣ OUT IN THE STREET ▣

'I remember skipping home from my Leeds primary school
every Monday dinner time to what was then my favourite meal –
cold beef sandwiches and Scotch pancakes. The kitchen would
be hot and steamy, and before eating I would have to turn the
mangle. The Scotch pancake man, as he was known to all the

All children loved a ride on the hay waggon – it was part of summer.

people who lived in Harehills, came round with a large basket, covered with a snowy tea towel, in which were layers of these mouth-watering treats. Smothered in butter, they were the highlight of my week.

Other memories include the man who came round with his horse and cart selling firewood, or chips as we called them. Often he would let us clamber on top of the sticks and take us for a ride round to his next stop. Then there was the piper. He was an institution. I remember hearing his penny whistle during the last lesson at Notre Dame, when I, as a ten-year-old, was high up in the biology lab overlooking Woodhouse. He must have walked for miles, piping out his tunes, tunes both happy and plaintive, and we always ran out when he came round our streets. He would give me a big smile when he accepted the pennies (and often the bit of home baking) my mother always sent out to him.

But best of all was the one man band. I can see and hear him now, running along the street, playing a mouth organ, with drums, cymbals and various other instruments attached, by what seemed to me miraculous means, to almost every part of his anatomy. There was always a line of children running or skipping after him, and all the mums standing at their doors enjoying the spectacle, and putting pennies into his tin mug.

There were no gangs as such in those days, but all the children used to play together at the end of the street. I can sympathise now with the owners of the end house, with its big wall, which was used for all our ball games, yet they never complained. We played Queenie, Stand All, Kick Out Ball, and just before it got dusk and the street lamps came on, one of our favourite games was Kicking Lamp Posts. These were set to come on at a certain time, but if one kicked the post hard enough one could upset the balance and the lamp would come on a few minutes before its due time. Our mothers would walk along to collect us, and stand chatting on the corner, whilst we would feel the thrill of still playing when it was almost dark.'

Two happy children from Shibden in the winter of 1953. Winston Churchill's 'Siren Suit' was still being copied – in this case as an outdoor play suit.

▣ WINTER GAMES ▣

'How did we amuse ourselves on winter evenings in those long-ago days before television? Quite well, actually.

Of course, there was radio, with Uncle Mac, Auntie Doris and Larry the Lamb in *Children's Hour*. There were also the Ovaltinies on Radio Luxembourg on Sunday afternoons. I joined the Ovaltinies, and had to endure some teasing after I had innocently asked if I could have a new dress when it was my turn to join in on the radio. I was only about seven at the time, and didn't realise that Johnny, Winnie and Elsie were the voices of one man.

Before 1939 the lamplighter would come round to light the gas lamp outside our house. After tea we would play beneath it. Hopscotch, using a flat stone or an old broken tile, Grandmother's Footsteps, hide and seek, kick the can. Also, I am ashamed to say, knocking on doors and running away. Sometimes there would be as many as ten of us playing leapfrog all the way down the street. No danger from cars in those days, none of our neighbours had one. No danger, either, from strangers enticing us away.

My mother didn't go out to work, and had time to play Snap or Beggar my Neighbour. We also played paper and pencil games such as noughts and crosses, which nowadays seem to require complicated and expensive equipment. Sometimes my friend from next door would come to tea, or I would go there. She and her sisters had a huge doll's house, made by one of her uncles. It even had electric lights. On special occasions we were allowed to play with the whole house, under supervision. But mostly we were only allowed to choose the furniture from one room to play with on the baking board. If it was Monday evening, we had to go in the kitchen while her father listened to *Monday Night at Eight* on the radio.

When the war started in 1939 we had the black-out and no gas lamps. I don't remember playing outside in those days. We had just moved house and there was no gas lamp outside, so it wouldn't have been the same.

Indoors, we played board games such as ludo, snakes and ladders, Chinese chequers. I enjoyed many games of draughts with my father. In vain I would try to beat him, but usually ended up trapped in a corner of the board, moving across the same two squares, hoping he would take pity on me and let me out.

I had a bagatelle board and at Christmas when my cousin came we would have a competition with this, or we played table tennis on the dining table. I also spent many happy hours with my nose in a book. I would sit in the armchair, in front of the coal fire, lost to the world. My mother would call from the kitchen, "Nancy, put some coal on the fire", or "Nancy, does the fire need mending?" I wouldn't hear. Many times I dreamed until the fire went out.'

▣ GAMES WE PLAYED ▣

'When I was about twelve, I had to wash five steps and some of the pavement every Saturday morning. A boy used to come and torment me and step on the clean steps, so one day I clouted him with the wet floorcloth without wringing it out first. We later became the best of friends!

When we went to the fruiterer's we would pay ½d or 1d for the straw rope which was tied round the cases. Then we would sling this rope over the crossbar on the lamp post and swing on it. Sometimes we tied it high up onto the lamp post and then we would swing round the lamp post and back again.

Some children had celluloid dolls but many parents couldn't afford them, so instead the children had a peg on which they drew a face. Dressmakers would give the children pieces of material – lace, satin, velvet etc and we would make it into coats and dresses to dress the dolls. A piece of crimson velvet was a real treasure.

Games played included whip and top – on the top we chalked coloured rings and when spinning it gave pretty colours and patterns; hopscotch on the pavement – we marked it out with chalk or sandstone. Sometimes we played checks and taws (marbles). There were several checks which were a half inch cube. We scrambled (or threw) the checks and then threw up the taw and attempted to pick up first one, then two and then three checks etc at a time before catching the taw. We used to play this knelt down on the flags.

For dolly parties we used a piece of old rug, a chair or stool. We ground some sandstone and pretended it was tea, milk and sugar.

On the way to school we would call at the fruiterer's and buy some liquorice for ½d. It was proper yellow root liquorice which we chewed until it became like thick straw. Sometimes we had

Dr Tanner Sticks which were very hard and like liquorice. We broke these into pieces to make it last and put it in our mouth. On picnics we put a piece in a lemonade bottle with water, shook it up really well and called it Spanish Wine.

We bought balls of cork wool for 1d which was coloured and sometimes variegated, which was very special. With four nails on a wooden bobbin we made a long length and then wound it round and round and stitched it. I once made a dressing table set for my Auntie.'

'My cousin and myself were often the only two girls playing with a gang of boys, and being the youngest were just tolerated by the boys since one of them was my brother. A popular game was "tin can squash". We played this on spare land near to an old wall and the garages of my father and uncle's haulage business, some hen huts and a rough unmade stoney lane. The game was a version of hide and seek, but one of the hiders had to kick an old tin can from near the wall as far as possible down this lane, and everyone except the "seeker" ran to hide. The seeker had to retrieve the can and return to the starting point before looking for the "hiders". The people hiding had if possible then to get back to where the tin was without being caught by the seeker. Being mere girls, Sheila and myself were unable to kick the can very far, which didn't give us enough time to hide, so we soon got fed up and left the boys to play by themselves.'

'In the 1930s at Birdsedge we used to buy rope from the greengrocer's which came from orange boxes for one penny and used it for skipping ropes. In the summer holidays we would take large pieces of cardboard to a steep field which was called "The Roly Poly Field" and slide down on the cardboard – it was the highlight of our holiday. Most boys had iron hoops called "bullies" and girls would use an old bicycle wheel and a stick to hit it with.'

'As a child in the 1940s I think that the winters seemed to be harder than now. We were able to go sledging every year and when the river flooded the water froze hard enough for those with ice-skates to enjoy themselves. Children didn't wear trousers, girls wore skirts and the boys wore short pants. Knee socks instead of ankle socks were the only concession to cold as far as our legs were concerned. Thighs got very chapped and the agony of getting into the bath is well remembered. The only salves were thick oil based ones like zinc and castor oil cream or Vaseline. These soothed eventually but applying them was messy and uncomfortable.

When the weather improved the hoops came out – we called them bowls ("ow" as in town) and they were propelled along by hitting them with a short stick. There was little traffic so we could race round the village roads without interruption or danger. Next came whips and tops, the tops were decorated with patterns in coloured chalks so they looked pretty when spinning. Again, we raced along the roads to see who could keep the top spinning longest. Skipping ropes, then marbles were the next phase in the playing ritual.'

▣ PARTY TIME ▣

'Birthday and Christmas parties between the wars were very different to today. We were sent invitations about two weeks ahead and we had to write formal replies – "So-and-so thanks so-and-so for her kind invitation to be present at her party on (date) and has much pleasure in accepting". However small the house, parties were mostly held at home, although one or two of my wealthier friends might hire a hall. The games we played were very tame, I suppose; Oranges and Lemons, Here We Come Gathering Nuts in May and so on. My mother produced some lovely teas. As well as jellies we had "candlesticks" – rings of pineapple with half a banana fixed into the hole and a piece of chocolate stuck in the top for a "wick"; and "poached eggs" – an apricot half on a round piece of sponge cake surrounded by whipped cream.'

SCHOOLDAYS – THE BEST YEARS OF OUR LIVES?

Long walks to school in all weathers, coal fires in the classrooms, strict discipline and hard times – some of the memories shared by generations of Yorkshire children.

▣ WE ALL WALKED TO SCHOOL ▣

'I went to Thurstonland endowed school, which catered for all local children from five to 14. Everyone walked to school, some from two miles away. They all bought a packed lunch and a paper twist of cocoa and sugar in the winter. The infants' teacher would boil a pan on top of the coal stove and the steaming mugs of cocoa were passed round the circle of eager children and then topped off with a spoonful of condensed milk.'

▣ TIP-UP SEATS AND INKWELLS ▣

'At Chapelthorpe in the 1920s we had tip-up seats and inkwells – a lad would mix the ink and fill the inkwells, which were filthy. There was no talking in class or it was the cane given by the class teacher or, much worse, to be sent to the headmaster. Boys and girls were always separated and even at playtime had to come out of different doors and their playground was divided by a wall. We had to walk to school, back home for dinner, school again and then home at teatime. Those who lived too far away to get home for dinner would make a pot of cocoa for a penny. If your parents could afford it you could get a small bottle of milk for a halfpenny.'

BOARD OF EDUCATION.

Form 146a. (1).

SCHEDULE III.

Local Education Authority York* (W.R) Ad. Co

LABOUR CERTIFICATE, NO. 1 (a) (for total exemption after 13 years of age).

AGE AND EMPLOYMENT.

———

I CERTIFY that *Frank Mitchell*,

residing at *Tissnshaw Farm, Oak.*,

was on the 23rd day of *July* 1920, not

less than **thirteen** years of age, having been born on

the 28th day of *June*, 1907, as appears

by the Registrar's Certificate [~~or the Statutory Declaration~~]

now produced to me, and has been shown to the satisfac-

tion of the local education authority for this district to be

beneficially employed.

(Signed) *Burcah*,

(¹) or other officer.   (¹) Clerk to the Local Education Authority.

(1654) Wt. 18860—883o 40,000 9/19 J. T. & S., Ltd. 162   [P.T.O.
(854) Wt. 36295—1117o 40,000 2/20 J.T. & S., Ltd. 162

A Labour Certificate issued in 1920 enabling young Frank Mitchell to be employed full time at the age of 13. His teacher certified he had attended school at least 350 times over five years.

▨ I Suppose it Did us Good ▨

'At Holmfirth just after the First World War we learned to count by reciting times tables and by counting little pot beans, and to read by reciting the alphabet and then stringing the letters together.

We always knew what sort of mood the headmaster was in by the colour of his suit. We had quite an old teacher, she never caned anyone but she used to pretend she was going to give you a clout across the head; we were never sure if we were going to get it or not.

We used to have religious studies and the vicar used to come to take us for them. He didn't have a roof to his mouth so we had great difficulty understanding what he was saying. He must have got very frustrated by this and used to hit us on the head because we couldn't answer his questions.

The pupils who were undernourished had to go to the teacher's room at morning play time and were made to drink a mug of reconstituted dried milk which had globules of fat floating on top, also a spoonful of cod liver oil had to be taken. It was awful but I suppose it did us all good.'

▨ Pinafore and Dress ▨

'When I started school at five years old I was terrified to see so many children, 54 in my class. But the teacher soon gave you a sense of security because she was completely in charge of the situation. Over my dress I wore a pinafore, which kept our dresses clean, and when we got home we had to take off both the dress and pinafore and change into our playing clothes. I suppose the type of material from which our dresses were made was not so easy to wash before washing machines appeared. We had new dresses for Sunday only, which became school dresses in time. Sometimes our school dresses had become very short and had to have false hems put on so as not to be indelicate!'

▨ Apples and Boots ▨

'I remember at Castleton school the poor children being called out to the front of the class for cod liver oil and malt. They also got a free apple and some got "Boots for Bairns". Unemployment was rife then.'

▣ Cuts and Nits ▣

'We lived within ten minutes walk of Cutsyke school and started going at the age of five. I left at the age of 13 in 1925, a little sooner than most of my classmates. Being a strong healthy child, I was first choice to stay at home and help my Mum who became increasingly unwell and in need of support. In the eight years I was on the register, I could not have attended for more than half of the time and that was mostly during the early years. From the age of eight or nine I was too busy to attend school; valuable at home, baking and washing, cooking and cleaning. I probably saw as much of Mr Black, the school "bobby", as some of the teachers. I don't think I was present for long enough at a time to learn how to learn; to make use of books, understand the grammar or put down the ideas I did possess with the appropriate spelling. The regular teachers appreciated my position and tended to make use of my domestic talents instead of trying to instil a formal education. Once, Mrs Cobb spilt milk on her tray cloth and I spent the whole morning working on that stain, soaking it in milk, until it was barely visible. To me, this was a morning well spent but it did not help my education. Sometimes, the teachers would make me look foolish in front of the class. I remembered everything I was taught by my mother but little of what I was taught in school. She did not need a stick to drive in the information.

A new teacher asked me. "Where's Yorkshire?" and I politely and truthfully replied, "This is Yorkshire, Sir, where we live." He must have been expecting a reply which indicated a greater understanding of geography as he dragged me to the front of the class and subjected me to such ridicule that the whole class laughed at me. Then he made me make a fist and with the edge of two rulers together, he brayed the knuckles of both my hands so hard that I wet myself with the pain. I met my Dad on the way home at lunchtime and by now my hands were so bruised and

Stanbury Primary School around 1914. Even the scruffiest of the boys is wearing shiny clogs. (Below) Central Infants School, Heckmondwike in 1938.

swollen that I could neither open nor close them. When he saw them he took me straight back to school and demanded to see the teacher, who said he hadn't realised that he had hit me so hard. Dad said that he needed a bit of cooling off and picked him up and dunked him head first in the rain barrel. Dad made it quite clear that he would regret it if ever there was any further trouble. I was unable to use my hands for a week and Mum had to feed me all my meals.

After this my attendances at school became more infrequent as Mum struggled to cope with raising a family and looking after a home. However, my name stayed on the school register so the school bobby found it necessary to come looking for me. My Mum was always very apologetic and said she had had to keep me at home that day for whatever reason and he would ask her to make sure I went the next day but they both knew the realities of the situation.

The school bobby also made quarterly visits with the school nurse who was checking heads for a different purpose. At arm's length and with the aid of two knitting needles, she would lift up the hair and stare closely at the head underneath. The class was then divided into two groups – the first was sent back to work and the second was told to "wait there". I was never in this second group but it always frightened me. My friend Hilda was often included in the chosen few, who were in the minority. I sat behind her in school and had seen the creepy-crawlies which she carried in her hair – climbing to the surface, over the next tuft of hair, and then burrowing down again into another gap. At times there were several insects moving about at the same time, all busying themselves with their unspeakable activities.

The school nurse would take a small amount of hair from the top of the head and comb a piece forward. Then with large scissors and a minimum of finesse, she would hack away at the hair behind letting it fall in untidy clumps into the waste paper basket. After the scissors came the pomade – an ointment made from apples supposedly but more closely resembling a mixture of vaseline and tar. The evil-smelling mixture was plastered onto the stubble which was all that remained of the hair. The piece that had been combed forward was now pulled back, ostensibly to hide the ravages behind, but there was no possible way of hiding the devastation or the shame. Not the discovery of head lice, which we considered an environmental problem (although we didn't know the term), but the loss of one's hair was a loss of dignity, of femininity and pride; things which would not grow back in a few short weeks. Each child was given a note to take home which said the nurse had been "distressed to find your child with a lousy head which necessitated the treatment which had been applied".

We were always very frightened that it might be our turn next time but my Mum always reassured us and said it could not happen to us because she took such great care of our hair. "Never let anyone else use your hat and never put on anyone else's," she would insist. Every night she brushed and combed our hair until it shone and then she would do it "just once more".

In 1925 Mrs Cobb, my teacher, sent a note to my Mum inviting me to attend a party she was giving for everyone who was leaving even though I had not always been able to attend very often. My Mum remembered some velvet which my uncle had bought and managed to make a lovely dark green dress which I thought was the most beautiful dress there ever was. There was not enough material for sleeves but that did not matter – Mum acquired some gold braiding which lifted the dark colour and added a luxurious touch. It also helped to eke out the material so that it did not appear skimped but nobody else would have known. My Mum let me wear her mother's pearls, "just this once". It was a wonderful party and I felt like the belle of the ball and thought my dress was above everyone else's.'

▧ OAK APPLE DAY ▧

'At Scholes, and elsewhere, if you did not go to school on Oak Apple Day with a piece of oak twig or a leaf pinned to your clothing you were chased by "Apple boys" brandishing stinging nettles and just waiting to use them.'

'When I first started school, we still used shells to count and sand trays to write, also slates, and we learned to knit and sew at a very early age. At ten years old we were sent to the local grammar school to sit for our "County/Minor Scholarship". If we passed this exam then we attended the grammar school (this, by the way, was not compulsory) until we were 16 or 18 years old, or we stayed at elementary school up to the age of 14.

One of the happiest days of our year was undoubtedly Whit Monday when after lunch we all went to church for a short service and then assembled outside for our Whit walk. In our small village we could not afford a band as the large Sunday schools did. We visited several big houses and sang hymns. The gentry sat outside – it was always sunny – and as we left we were given a new penny each; at some houses we were also given sweets and fruit. After a sandwich and bun tea in the school room we had races on the village green – known as the Park in our village. The Sunday school superintendent who was also our wealthy patron would hand out prizes to the winners. Each year a tin trunk of toys would be brought and the contents displayed on a table, each winner was allowed to choose their own prize.

The other major event in our life at school was the "Prize Giving". During the afternoon we would all be sent out to play, this was always just before Christmas. When we were allowed back into the school the partition would have been folded back and chairs arranged in neat rows. Seated on the platform was the wife of the local Squire and "Miss Dolly" who ran the Sunday school (another wealthy woman). Each child was given a present. If a year of complete attendance had been completed an extra prize of a book was also given by the lady from the Hall, Mrs Fisher. My brother was allowed to attend school full time for a few weeks even though he was only three years old in order to qualify for a prize, I think his present was a fire engine.

The school concert was an annual event, as was the "Married Ladies' Effort" and the "Men's Effort". Our life centred around the school and church. The headmistress, Miss Grainger, gave each child who passed their county minor exam a half crown, an enormous sum in those days. It was considered a great thing to

A May Day procession at Rawdon in 1936.

pass for Honley (Holme Valley grammar school) but there was no disgrace in failing the exam.'

◼ THE MAY DAY PARADE ◼

'It was all systems go on the evening of 30th April in the 1930s when I was at infants' school. Prams, bicycles and scooters had to be trimmed with crêpe paper for the May Day parade round the school yard. For those with neither pram, bicycle or scooter, a hoop or maybe a doll had to suffice.

Usually two colours were used with strips woven through the spokes of the wheels, round handle bars and any other surface that could be covered. Much debate took place about colours, but it often came down to what the corner shop could provide. The results were splendid and mothers, and sometimes fathers too (as this was a time of large scale unemployment) looked on with pride as their youngsters pedalled and pushed round the concrete playground. We trotted home at the end of the afternoon sorry it was over and wanting to keep the decorations on forever.

111

Did it never rain on May Day or has time and memory painted an over rosy picture of what, to us children, was one of the magic moments of the year?'

◪ AT SECONDARY SCHOOL ◪

'The first secondary schools were built around 1935–36 for children who were unlucky enough not to pass the eleven plus exam. I was one of those children.

The secondary school was quite different to the old school – we had cookery lessons and housewifery and needlework, so called practical lessons. I remember one housewifery lesson we had was a wash day, if we did not take anything to wash the teacher would usually bring something of hers, usually her bloomers, and I do mean bloomers! As I had not taken anything I had nothing to iron so I offered to help my friend with some of hers. She gave me some silk French knickers to iron which belonged to her older sister. I, thinking the iron was cool, started with the leg and to my horror the whole motif came away with the iron. I was sent scurrying to the sewing room to see what could be done but sad to say I had to go home with my friend and explain to her mother what had happened. Fortunately for me, she was very kind about it. I never found out what her sister said, nothing good I don't suppose. I met her a long time after and we laughed about it.

We had a good headmaster at the school but we also had a deputy head. Her name was Alice Bacon, later to become MP for Leeds. She was quite handy with a cane, as I found to my cost once or twice. Talking in her class was not allowed.

In 1939, war was declared and our school was taken over for the fitting and distribution of gas masks to everyone in the town, so it was closed until December. By that time I had had my 14th birthday so I left and did not go back.'

◪ FROM FROEBELIAN SCHOOL TO LAWNSWOOD HIGH ◪

'I started school at the age of five years at the Froebelian school in Horsforth, so called because of the Froebel training of one of the founder teachers; this school is still flourishing today. We were happy there and the teaching was a good preparation for our further education. Two things stick in my mind. One was that we had dancing lessons which I hated; it has left me with a lifelong dislike of ballet. The other thing I remember was our weekly visit to Bramley baths and our walk back down Newlay Lane in a crocodile! For one penny we could buy a bar of "Bovril chocolate" from a vending machine at the baths and my friend and I used to have a competition to see if we could make it last till we got back to school.

The Leeds Girls' Modern school, which my grandmother and mother (who had been head girl in 1908) had attended was in Leeds. When the school moved to Lawnswood and was renamed Lawnswood High School in September 1931, I started in the kindergarten; I was transferred to the junior school on my first day, thanks, I am sure, to the small classes at the Froebelian. (Classes in the local elementary schools were often between 50 and 60 pupils.)

Although the girls who lived near school went home for their lunch, those of us who lived a distance away had to stay for our dinner at school. This cost 9d a day and on Monday it was always roast beef, two veg and apricot tart. Although there were nine girls on each table, the tart was cut quickly by the prefect at the head of the table into eight and then a mad dash to the kitchen to get another tart for "seconds". There was also a choice of sago and/or rice-not very popular!

One lunch time in 1937/8 one of the staff rushed in saying "get outside quickly girls there is a Zeppelin going over." We had a wonderful view of it. (It was always assumed afterwards that it was a reconnaissance trip and they were taking aerial photographs.) There was another occasion when we were at Guides when it came over Horsforth. It seemed to be enormous and very low over the houses, rather exciting to children who didn't think about the more sinister reason for it being there.

Progression through the school was without incident but I did regret later the lack of availability to study the sciences. We had a choice of either chemistry or biology but not both; we did no physics whatsoever at School Certificate level. This was in marked contrast to the Leeds Girls' High School which had a better science department and since the fees for the two schools were the same it would have been better, in hindsight, if I had transferred, but I don't think any of us thought of it.

The one teacher who stands out in my mind taught us Latin. She was well ahead of her time, teaching what I think is now called the direct approach. Our first lesson started with her introducing herself and saying, "From now on when I come in you will say 'Salve o Magistra' and I shall reply 'Salve o Puellae.'" She then started talking in Latin and if I remember correctly didn't speak a word of English for 40 minutes, a lot of which I can remember, 60 years later. I think of her now with a great deal of respect but at the time we were terrified of her, perhaps that is another reason for the impact she made on me.

Further education for girls was not encouraged before the war. Those who did stay in the sixth form and took Higher School Certificate frequently went to a teacher training college. However, two girls in the form above me were going to university, one to read biology and the other medicine and so I was able to do some classes with them, otherwise I had lessons on my own with the teacher.

One unbelievable fact was as follows: the boys' school was next door, separated by the swimming baths, but though there was no such barrier on the playing fields, there was, however, an invisible one, and if one knocked a ball onto the boys' area one had to find a prefect to find a boys' prefect to retrieve the ball! I might say this rule was often broken and I have often wondered if the rule was fabricated by the prefects who, no doubt, had boy friends at the boys' school.

The headmistress was only appreciated in hindsight and I for one have much to thank her for. I did as little work as possible, spending far too much time on the playing fields, so I was very shaken when she told me I wouldn't pass School Certificate and was too young to go into the sixth form. From that day I set out to prove her wrong.'

THE WORLD OF WORK

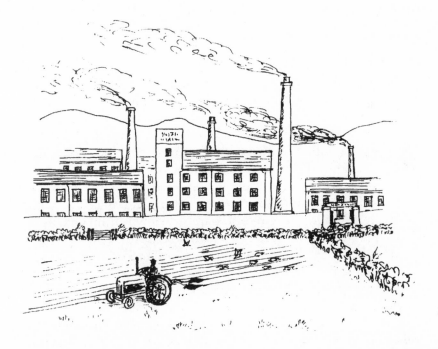

ON THE LAND

It is not so long since the working horse provided the power on the land, and farming had hardly changed since the century before. Many families have made their living from the land, a way of life which could be hard and unforgiving but which also gave great satisfaction and a sense of community.

◈ MORE THAN A PASSING INTEREST ◈

'I started taking more than a passing interest in farming when visiting my uncle, aunt and cousin in 1923 when I was ten years old. They milked cows twice a day early morning and late afternoon. These were hand milked into a pail, kept for that purpose, the milk was then emptied through a Syle cloth which acted as a sieve, this was tied round the neck of a ten gallon can or churn. In winter the animals were tied up by the neck to a stake and fed hay and given water. During milking they would be given flaked maize, oats and barley, that was from October to April, in other months the cows would be turned out to grass.

After breakfast the Galloway (type or breed of horse) was harnessed to the milk float, the churn, delivery can and half pint and one pint measures were put in the milk float and away my uncle would go on his delivery round locally. In the school holidays I would also go along with my cousin. The same was repeated in the afternoon. The milk was still warm, that is how the customers wanted it – they knew it was fresh milk.

From mid June to the end of July two Irish men, father and son, came to do the haymaking. They lived in the house. The hay fields were opened up using a scythe and round the bottom of the walls a horse-drawn machine cut the grass. It was then left, hoping the sun would shine and make hay with a bit of help from the men who strewed the grass around the field. When the grass was made into hay it was collected onto waggons and

116

On the milk round in 1931 – the farm did well in the Yorkshire Clean Milk competition that year.

taken to the barn where it was stored for winter use. When it rained the men lime-washed the cow sheds out, also the pig sties. There were always a few pigs on the farm. A barrel of beer was bought for the men to drink at 'lowance time along with bread and cheese.

During the Bradford holiday week, the mills shut down, less milk was sold and the surplus milk was put into shallow bowls and left to stand overnight, then the cream was skimmed off and put into a butter churn and made into butter, usually on a Tuesday following.

In 1930 I started going to a farm a bit nearer home and a bit bigger in size, where more cows were kept and two men delivered milk from May to September twice a day, October to April once a day. This farm went in for the Yorkshire Clean Milk competition and just got a mention. They were determined to do better in 1931 and they did. This entailed the utmost cleanliness

Old fashioned milking units at Cockleshaw farm in the mid-1950s – but we were happy!

and dedication to working with cows. The cows' udders and sides were clipped short at regular intervals, also tails trimmed. This helped to keep them clean. The udders were washed before every milking, the fore milk was drawn off into a container. The cows were hand-milked into dome-shaped stainless steel pails; the milk was strained into a ten gallon can or churn then taken and stood in a well of running water until it was time to go on the milk round. The two delivery cans had a half pint and one pint measure, each government stamped. Before milking began hands were scrubbed, a white cap covered the head, white coveralls covered the body, strapped round the top of the leg; these were washed twice a week. Spot checks and samples of milk were taken. All utensils that came in contact with milk were sterilized daily, a bit primitive but it worked. A fire was lit under a set pot in the washhouse; when the water boiled a galvanized container holding the utensils was put over the steam and left for perhaps 15 to 20 minutes. Cows were in either single or double standings, these had to be regularly scrubbed out. A silver rose bowl held for a year and silver medals to keep were awarded at the end of the competition for clean milk – a great honour. Hard work but it was worth it, it brought more milk customers.

In 1934 my husband and I rented our first farm, twelve acres. There were two milk cows, one horse, a family of pigs and 50 laying hens and some equipment. All lighting was by paraffin lamps. The first cow we bought from Otley Auction Mart cost £13 plus carriage for having it delivered, although I can well remember animals being walked from Skipton and Otley. The landlord enlarged the buildings to hold eight cows, and learning from the farm already described we aimed to produce milk hygienically. In 1936 we started filling bottles with a jug. Just before the war in 1939, we bought what was called a two up and two down machine, which still had to be used manually. In the summer of 1939 electricity was brought to the farm, but in September all lights had to be blacked out, so it did not make much difference until after the war finished. We did have a milking machine on a three months trial but it never seemed to work properly so had it taken out and we went back to hand milking.

Double summer time was introduced from April to September. I think it made us all a bit lazy, you got up two hours before sunrise, you could not go into the hayfields to work the grass until the dew had gone, but then you would be working until eleven o'clock at night. All topsy turvy.

A War Agricultural (War Ag) Committee was formed nationwide; they were to help farmers plan to get the most out of the farms. No new machinery was available, and we were still very much dependent on the horse and horse-drawn machinery and hand labour. There was the Women's Land Army to help you out in a difficult time. The industrial north is not the best place to grow wheat, oats, barley, peas and sugar beet, the growing season is much too short. There was one summer when the oats ripened; they were cut with a horse-drawn binder, the sheaves stooked in the field then led to a corn rick to be thatched and wait for the thresher to come round. The thresher was drawn by a very old tractor, neighbouring farmers came to give a

Open Day on East Manywells Farm in the late 1950s attracted hundreds of visitors.

helping hand and you also got spectators enjoying an unusual scene in those parts. The government asked you to produce more and more milk and anything eatable, that included pigs, poultry and eggs.

Water was always a problem, many times we had to stay up until midnight to fill jugs and pans for use in the house. The cows drank from a water course which ran under a wall bottom down a field. A galvanized tank was fixed in the roof space and the water started running in to the tank about midnight so there was enough for the following day. We were able to put a steam boiler in enabling us to sterilize all the milking utensils. In the winter months sugar beet pulp had to be soaked overnight to feed to the cows at midday. During the last week of January 1947 it started to snow and freeze, it lasted until the end of March. There were two motors trapped by the snow for six weeks until the thaw set in. The road was a switchback, the snow fell, then drifted and then froze solid. Needless to say, the water froze solid, nothing we could do about that, so it was back to drawing water out of a well with a bucket.

The summer of 1947 was a good hay making time. A tractor came round with a stationary baler which was made good use of; the bales of hay were tied with wire. More machinery was coming onto the market; the first tractor we had was a secondhand Allis Chalmers.

We moved to a larger farm in the 1950s that had been neglected. Over a number of years the grass land was ploughed out and reseeded with better strains of grass seed that meant more hay, and that led to a hay baler and new tractors.

A "muck midden" was in a corner of the yard; the cow sheds and pig sties were cleaned out twice a day and now and again the poultry houses were also cleaned out, it was just like a compost heap. During March it had all to be taken on to the grass land by horse and cart. It was pulled out of the cart into heaps with a muck drag, a long-handled fork. It was then "scaled" or spread out with an ordinary fork. The fields were then draized or chain harrowed to get rid of the debris. Muck is now spread with a tractor and spreader usually filled by a hydraulic bucket.

In the late 1950s, in conjunction with the then Milk Marketing Board and June Dairy Festivals committee, farmers were encouraged to open their farms to the general public. About 1,000 visitors went to one farm on a Sunday afternoon to see the workings of a typical dairy farm.'

▓ ON THRESHING DAY ▓

'As a young child on my father's farm at Guiseley in the 1940s, I remember threshing day. Threshing had to be finished in one day, so all the local farmers would help each other carry out this momentous task. About a dozen men would arrive at our farm and when the work was finished at the end of the day, the womenfolk would make a meal for everyone, usually beef and Yorkshire pudding. The men would sit round a large table outside, and I would stand and stare.'

'It was said that the chaff from threshing day was very healthy to

Harry Hemingway and a loaded hay cart in 1942, and Joyce and her brother at Old Wood Farm.

Using a horse-drawn harvester in 1946.

have in a baby's mattress.'

◈ OLD WOOD FARM ◈

'My father brought my brother and me to Old Wood Farm in 1941, along with the housekeeper, a necessity for a farmer without a wife. The farm was on a lane which was reputed to be an old Roman road. We were very close to Rombalds Moor, and had beautiful views of Baildon Moor, a fact not appreciated by me at that time. I would have preferred houses nearby and other children to play with. I would have been about eight years old and my brother just four.

The house had been built in the 17th century. The floors were all stone flags and the cooking and washing facilities were very primitive. I was fortunate to have my own bedroom with whitewashed walls and a view of the sky through the small window. One morning, after visitors had been to see us the previous day, I was told to empty the ash from the fireplace in the parlour. The previous night must have been extremely cold because, when I pulled the front cover away, I saw a family of mice nesting in the warm ash. They scurried for the exit, through the kitchen, to the outside door. I was delighted to hear the housekeeper scream.

When I was not at school I spent most of the daylight hours working on the farm. Dad was exempt from the army as he was a farmer, but he was expected to grow produce which was not appropriate for the type of soil in this area, such as carrots and turnips. My job was to weed the rows of vegetables, returning to the house when I heard the sound which meant that dinner was ready.

In the summer, Dad used a horse-drawn mowing machine to cut the grass. Everyone had to work in the field, spreading the hay then, with a wooden rake, turning it into rows and finally into piles ready to be carted into the barns. Dad worked with a scythe cutting the grass around the edge of the field which could not be reached by the mowing machine. We also grew oats; when these were cut and tied into bundles, I had to prop the bundles upright in pairs to dry in the sun. At the end of the day, the inside of my arms looked as if I had a severe case of chickenpox. The farmers hired a combine harvester which was driven to each farm in turn. This was modern machinery, noisy, belching out clouds of foul smelling smoke but it was an enormous help in harvesting, separating the corn from the chaff and the straw. I found it fascinating with all the moving parts, but Dad would not let me go near it.

It may be a surprise to read that my favourite occupation was looking after the pigs. We had a large piggery with a tin roof and a number of pens inside. The building was warmer than the house and the pigs did not hit me. I watched them a great deal, they tended to do their mess in the corner away from their troughs. I removed the mess, I shovelled it into the barrow and soon learned that it was not wise to fill it too full as I could not wheel it to the tip. The little piglets were delightful, I watched them playing for as long as I was able. Unfortunately I was never allowed to see them being born. The housekeeper said it was rude and not the right thing for a girl to see. Dad kept another, much larger pig in a sty at the other end of the farm. He would not let me play with this one, but never told me why. We were supplied with potatoes dyed blue to indicate that they were unfit for human consumption. The pigs enjoyed them, though, so did I when I was keeping the fire going underneath the setpot where they were boiling.

In the autumn, some of the pigs were let out and I was told to take them across the field to the woods, where they could snuffle for beechmast and other things they could eat. They happily wandered all over, some became hidden in the undergrowth whilst others crossed the small beck. There were times when I thought I would never get them back to the farm. Fortunately, my friend the sheepdog was a great help in herding them together and driving them back to the piggery.'

— · —

MINING MEMORIES

— · —

Life in a close-knit mining community holds many memories – of work and of strikes, of danger and of friendship.

▣ WORK AND STRIKE ▣

'My father was a coal miner, as were his father and brothers. He started at the pit at Cutsyke at the age of twelve after a limited education at school at the turn of the century where he learnt to read, write and count. It was all he needed to dig coal out of the ground, count his tubs and sign for his pay. He was a coalface man working invariably under cramped, dirty and damp conditions, to hew seams of coal from the surrounding rock. Then he would scrape the coal back before shovelling it into the tubs which were carried to the surface. Each tub was about four feet square and held half a ton carried on little iron wheels which ran on a network of rails through the pit.

Every coalface man had his own tubs, on which would be chalked his own identifying number and payment at the end of the week was based on how many tubs he had filled. Each man employed a boy, known as a driver, to look after his tubs. He would link them together, and then harness the train to one of the pit ponies before hauling it through the tunnels to the cage and thence to the "top". But it was the "looking after" that was most important. Dad gave his driver £2 a week just to sit on the tubs and reckoned it was cheap at the price. If you looked after your boy, he looked after your tubs; it was not unknown for untended tubs to disappear. "I got eight tubs out today," my father would say, recounting the result of a hard shift. "Have you got eight?" "Aye Bill, I've got eight," the boy would confirm that they were all there and all marked with my Dad's number.

Every day they checked in the same way and no one ever touched my Dad's tubs. Once his driver told Dad he'd seen someone muttying – rubbing a miner's number off a tub, and replacing it with another. "Leave it to me, lad," my Dad had said, "and don't mention it to anyone." It was sound advice, in an intense situation. Feelings ran high when a miner had been robbed of the coal he had dug and the messenger was as likely to be clubbed with a shovel or pickaxe handle, as the one who'd been accused of the theft. Even my Dad, tough as he was, knew that it was something which must be handled with care. He called at the office at the end of the shift, sticking his head round the door but going no further in. He called loudly to my cousin Harry, making sure that everyone could hear: "Your Aunty would like a word, if you can call in after work." Then he rejoined the shift that was making its way out of the pit. Harry very rarely had occasion to speak to my Mum, and he knew that it must be his uncle who wanted a word in private. Harry called in, muttying was mentioned, and names were exchanged. From there the matter was handled by the main office. The thief was not allowed to get away with his crime, but no one was any wiser as to how the management found him out.

My Dad was proud of his ability to dig out coal and few others would get eight tubs in similar conditions. Since more coal meant more pay he must have had more to take home than most of his workmates, only he did not take the pay home – all but 30 shillings a week he kept to spend on drink.

Mining was a tough job. Coal had to be hacked out from beneath hundreds of feet of rock where it had lain compressed for thousands of years. It was done crouching, sometimes half-lying and there was no room for a full swing of the pick. Cutting tunnels in the rock increased the risk of a roof collapse and by altering the flow of underground streams it flooded areas which had previously been relatively dry. Mining was a continuous battle against water. Where there was coal there was gas – colourless, odourless methane gas which infiltrated the tunnels and robbed the miners of their oxygen supply. Or it increased in concentration to explosion point, when one spark from a pick glancing off the stone, could blast those working in the vicinity and bring down the roof. When disaster struck it did so quickly giving little time to escape. Miners were crushed under thousands of tons of stone or trapped unable to work free before the air ran out or water filled their cavern. Above ground, the unscheduled wail of the pit buzzer summoned the safety team to the pit and men from other shifts also came. Ambulances drawn by horses came from Castleford. Families and friends all came to wait and wail for news of their loved ones. After the emergency the pit returned to normal with men crawling about in the same tunnels where their mates had been maimed and mutilated. In some cottages life would never be normal again. Broken men would be propped up in a chair or their chairs would remain empty until sold by the widow who found it impossible to survive on a pension of ten shillings a week.

At the end of each shift men would nod to the cage-man in unspoken thanks for bringing them up safely and they would pass him their identification tags which confirmed that those who had gone down had also come up. The cage-man would often be an "old" miner who had been hurt down the pit and was now only fit for light duties. The men walked home still filthy but wearing walking clothes on top of the dirt. It was too hot in the pit to wear anything more than a pair of knee-length bannakers which in reality were little more than cut-down pyjama trousers. My Dad tied the bannakers to the belt of his trousers and when he reached home he would simply drop them on the scullery floor. Mum or I would then wash and dry them ready for the next day. He then had a bath, lifting the zinc bath which hung on the wall. The water was heated in the set-pot, a large cauldron set in bricks, before his return. When he shouted someone was required to scrub his back and this was often me. Although he never spoke to me about digging coal, when the seam was particularly narrow his back would be full of deep scratches which he insisted I scrubbed hard without regard for the discomfort it would cause in order to get the coal dust out.

I was only nine years old when the Great Coal Strike began. It was more than men being out of work – in Cutsyke the whole community was out of work. The knock-on effects were widespread in other areas because coal powered so many activities. It affected the trains and power stations. It powered our homes; it was our heat, light and cooking. It coloured our whole lives, our homes, our clothes and our faces. Its spoil built our hills and blotted out the light. On wet days it added browns as well as black to the rivulets which ran from the slag heaps and along the streets. Coal shaped and scarred our menfolk, bending them so regularly that it was more natural than standing up straight and breaking some of them so that they would never be able to stand at all. Coal dominated our womenfolk – they too were on shift work with the pattern of their day determined by the working of the pit, but there was no clocking off when the hooter sounded. When the last cage had come up women were still cooking, cleaning and scrubbing – always washing. The anger which was born and developed in sub-human conditions in the pit, where grown men crawled on bruised and bloody knees and arms and breathed and ate the dust which they were paid to create, boiled over when they reached home and they often lashed out on the women and children.

Few miners complained about the back-breaking work or the dust that was eroding their lungs and would shorten their old age as these were felt to be inevitable features of a miner's life. However, the refusal of the owners to employ a permanent man to look after the pumps, meant that the men underground were regularly in danger of drowning in a grave which they, themselves, were digging. It was this, more than wages, sick pay and holidays with pay which hardened the strikers' resolve. Safety was an issue which was not negotiable and the pits would stay closed until changes were made.

Ironically the strike forced the owners to keep the pumps going when the miners were not there or run the risk of losing the progress which had already been made. My Dad was a member of the safety team which went in every day to see to the pumps and this was recognised by the strikers as support for their aims. I don't know whether he was paid for this job but our monthly allocation of coal continued and I never went hungry which was more than most people in Cutsyke could claim.

Families were starving and selling their belongings to buy food, but with most of their neighbours in a similar position, few people could afford to buy and homes were broken up for a matter of shillings. Some miners did not join the strike and others were driven back to work by the grinding poverty and for a short time their efforts put food in their families' mouths but it was at horrendous expense. Blacklegs were met on the way home and stripped of the coal they were carrying and then beaten unmercifully by the more thuggish elements of their former workmates.

The pits continued to operate on a severely reduced scale but the output did not always reach its intended destination. At the end of our street was a high banking along which rail tracks carried trucks of coal from the pit. Some of the younger strikers became expert at climbing onto the moving trucks and tipping their contents just before Cutsyke Bridge. At the bottom of the banking many hands waited for the coal to roll down to them. It was quickly gathered and carried away, leaving little evidence that it had ever been there.

Most people supported the strike and stubbornly remained out through two years of near starvation. There was no help from the State for people who were said to have "voluntarily placed themselves in this position".

My Mum and Dad did what they could to ease the suffering

and Mum went to Castleford and Dad to Normanton to beg for food around the shops. I was left to make the bread, cutting the dough into six ounce balls for cobs instead of the usual two pound loaves. Mum returned with something from nearly every shop she had visited – lentils, pearl barley, split peas, half a stone of dried peas and lots of bones. The peas were put to steep, the fire lit under the set-pot in the scullery behind the kitchen and the bones put in to boil for hours. Dad returned with pigs' feet and sheeps' heads and after cleaning they went in with the bones. With my brother and sister, I cut into small cubes turnips, carrots and parsnips from Dad's allotment. The next day, after Mum and Dad had scraped all the bones, the vegetables were added to the set-pot. The broth was so rich, Mum removed a bucketful and replaced it with a bucket of water. The children began to queue up outside our back door from as far away as Glasshoughton. Every child had a cob of bread and half a pint pot full of broth. Anyone with a larger bowl was sent home for his or her father's pint pot.

Feeding children in this way continued twice a week until the strike was over and Mum's broth was often the only hot meal they got any day. The shopkeepers started to keep odds and ends of food for when Mum called and the butcher left a bit more meat on the bones.

During the strike the ponies were brought up from the pit bottom. They usually only saw daylight in August when they came up for a rest. The light, weather, diet and complete change of life proved too much for some and they were shot because they were said to have gone mad. Others were given blinkers and put out to graze in fields near the pit.

At the end of the strike the whole village went mad. Men and women hugged each other and tears of joy rolled like peas down their faces. A street party was held with both food and entertainment. Bunting was hung across every street and everyone joined in. After the men went back, sick pay was introduced, under strict controls and pensions were awarded to men unable to work following an injury down the pit. At last the owners were taking responsibility for the working conditions in which they expected their employees to toil.

The most obvious development was the erection of the pit

head baths which meant the men no longer had to put on their everyday clothes at the pit-head and make them dirty from the inside. No more walking through the streets with filthy hands and arms, faces and hair, bringing the dust from the coal-face into their own kitchens.'

◼ IN THE SHADOW OF THE PIT ◼

'I was born and spent my youth in Kinsley, a small mining community. We lived in the shadow of the pit and the "muck stack". My father was a miner, so we were never short of coal. The people who didn't work at the pit, though, often couldn't afford to buy coal. I can remember seeing men and women pushing old prams up the road to the slag heap to pick up bits of coal. It was a dangerous thing to do and it wasn't unheard of for the odd person to be killed doing it.

Ponies were used down the mines and as they worked in dark conditions for so long many of them were blind, or very nearly so. These poor animals were only brought up into the field once a year when the mines closed for the workers to have a holiday. Even when there was a holiday, we very rarely went away.

I remember my mother packing my dad's sandwiches (always home-made bread and jam) in a "snap" tin (a metal tin shaped like a slice of bread). He also took cold water in a "dudley", a round metal container.'

◼ THE KNOCKER UP ◼

'The time was half past four in the morning and the sound of the pit buzzer could be heard in every home in the village. Almost at the same time the tapping of the "knocker up" could be heard as he tapped on the bedroom windows with a clothes prop. This service cost one penny a day, but it was worth it to the families who were reluctant to get out of bed, as he wouldn't go away until the occupants had opened the bedroom window and put out their heads to show they were awake.

After half an hour the first sound of clogs and pit boots could be heard passing down the street. The second buzzer was heard at ten minutes to six giving a warning that the last cage for the day shift would be going down the shaft in five minutes and latecomers would not be allowed to work that day.

The end of the shift was signalled by the sound of the buzzer at 2.15 pm and the men made their way to the lamp room to hand in identity checks and lamps. Again the sound of clogs and pit boots could be heard as the men hurried home.'

▨ AFTER THE SHIFT ▨

'Whether it was because they were so glad to be up in the fresh air after the shift, the men didn't always go straight home. They stopped on spare ground on the way for a game of "knurr and spell". A short piece of wood was balanced on a stone and struck with a wooden striker or long stick as far as possible.

On pay day the game was not so innocent. Pitch and toss, a gambling game, was played by groups of men, with a "lookout" for the policeman, because it was against the law to gamble on unlicensed premises. Some families suffered from this game by being short of housekeeping money. But the vast majority of miners were good family men and very proud of their sons and daughters who passed their "scholarship" to go to the grammar school.'

—·—

IN THE MILLS

—·—

Many went into the mills to work, straight from school.

▨ STRAIGHT FROM SCHOOL ▨

'I started work at twelve, before the First World War, and spent half a day at school and half a day in a cotton mill at Hightown. I received 2s 6d a week for half a week's work. A full week was 64 hours. We started work at 6 am and wore clogs and shawls and

C.W. Wade, the cloth dyer and finisher used this delivery lorry in the 1920s around Rawdon.

took sandwiches for breakfast and a tin can, with tea in. Outside where we worked there was a firing place with a big thing with holes in and the cans fitted in there. Half an hour before breakfast the Firing Man would put the heat on and the tea would be warmed.'

✣ LEARNING AS A "NIPPER" ✣

'Until the late 1970s the main industry in our two small towns of Guiseley and Yeadon was woollen textiles. This consisted of seven large mills which processed the cloth from raw wool to the finished product.There was a silk mill until approximately 1930, after closure it then became the well known Silver Cross pram factory. There were also four large dyeing and finishing mills as well as a number of small mills known as "ragoils" (holes) whose work consisted of pulling to shreds old cloth and rags which went into making poor quality cloth known as shoddy! The

A Yorkshire 'jigger' manufactured by Stead Bros. of Halifax and seen here at Moorhouse and Wainwrights' dyeworks near Horsforth.

forerunner perhaps of the modern recycling.

I myself had to learn weaving on leaving school at 14, along with many others. We were known as "Nippers". The noise in the old weaving sheds was horrendous. Until one became used to it after a day's work our ears did nothing but ring! In a short time, however, we did get used to it and in a few weeks would be able to hear and converse in an ordinary voice instead of shouting. Frequent were the clips we received about the head on not hearing what was said and causing us to make a mistake. The wage was seven shillings and six pence per week. Our starting time was 7 am to 5.15 pm with half an hour for breakfast and one hour for lunch, Monday to Friday, and Saturday mornings, 7 am until 11.45 am. Anyone arriving three minutes later than 7 am would find the main gates locked, this meant going to the small side door of the office and having your name taken by the staff. After 7.05 am the office door was closed and no worker allowed into the mill until 8.30 am.

The first lesson was how to tie a weaver's knot, start and stop the loom. On the old broadlooms this was no mean feat as the loom had to be brought into an upright position so the shuttle could be pushed right into what was known as the box. If this was not done correctly the loom would give an almighty bang, probably breaking part of the loom. Later on, with practice you became adept at pushing the shuttle into the box as the loom was moving. On becoming more skilled you learned how to catch the shuttle and throw the replacement into the box. You had to be careful how you caught a moving shuttle as I personally saw an experienced weaver of 30 years try and stop the shuttle with hand pointing the wrong way, resulting in the shuttle taking his hand part way into the box and removing one finger at the first joint and the tip of another. That lesson went home and stayed with me!

Another important lesson that had to be learned was how to read a pattern of the cloth, so that if, as so often happened, a number of warp threads broke in a bunch, you were able to thread the ends on the correct shafts, otherwise the design on the cloth was ruined. Various labouring jobs also came our way, such as going to the weft department with empty bobbins and exchanging them for a basket full of weft. Another task was the cleaning, known as fettling! Each Saturday morning at 11 am the driving force of the looms was shut down allowing three quarters of an hour to clean. Often this was not long enough to reach the standard required so we had to learn (not by the rules) how much could be done whilst the looms were running. This meant wiping moving parts with a cloth, brushing rapidly with a hand brush at the dry fluff known as fud. We then crawled underneath doing as much as possible, again whilst dodging the moving parts, then when the looms did stop there was time to clean the parts that could not be done before. The cleanings were then swept into a pile and sorted, fud and reasonably clean cloth (or thrums) were put into one basket and the filth into another. These were then taken to another department to be checked, weighed and inspected to make sure that every re-usable scrap had been saved.

There were the usual accidents, the main two being caused by

Inside a tailoring factory at Leeds after the war.

the picking stick and flying shuttles. The picking stick that threw the shuttles back and forth on the old looms stood out quite a long way, a small miscalculation or lapse of concentration and you were hit hard. My worst one was a split head, not through any fault of my own but the result of escaping from the usual initiation ceremony of blackening a nipper's face with dirty grease. I was patched up by the first aider and had to promise to keep quiet about what had happened to avoid anyone losing their job. The danger I considered worst was the shuttles weighing about a kilo with a steel point at each end, they were deadly and completely unpredictable, it only needed a minor fault in the loom to throw it out resulting in it travelling at speed for yards. If you were lucky you saw it flash past you, if not you felt it! I saw two weavers struck with the actual point, one on the head resulting in a long stay in hospital, the other damaging an arm muscle which troubled him the rest of his life. I don't remember anyone not getting hit at some time or other with the wooden part of the shuttle, which would stun or badly daze a weaver. If anyone was off work for any length of time the weavers would have a collection for the family.

It was not all doom and gloom, we still had time for a few pranks. One was adjusting the weft fork, making the loom stop each time it was started. Another, which now I know was very dangerous, was slightly lifting the foot board causing the weaver to stumble. I'm not really sure about the good old days, but we were never bored!'

OTHER WAYS WE MADE A LIVING

There were dozens of other ways we made a living in the past and these are just a few memories of milk rounds and baking bread, of life in service and industrious villages.

▣ STOCKSMOOR AND THURSTONLAND PEOPLE ▣

'After the coming of the railway to our village of Stocksmoor, between 1874 and 1878, many changes were made. One local farmer began to send his milk in churns to Huddersfield by train. People were able to travel to Huddersfield, Holmfirth and Meltham, and so could take up a variety of occupations such as engineering, work in the chemical industry, shops or textile mills outside their immediate area.

At the nearby village of Thurstonland, a brickworks was opened for the manufacture of bricks for lining the many tunnels required on the route from Huddersfield to Sheffield. There was also a small tannery and a blacksmith.

In the local hamlet of Thunderbridge, a water-driven corn grinding mill was set up to meet the needs of local farmers. There was also a small works making ammonia, which was used by local housewives for washing blankets.

The village of Stocksmoor was part of the parish of St Thomas, Thurstonland. There were 19 farms in the village during my childhood, but now there is only one which is fully operational.

Between Thunderbridge and Farnley Tyas there was a 600 acre wooded estate which contained Storthes Hall. This became the property of the West Riding Asylums Committee in 1898 and buildings were added to provide accommodation for nearly 350 mental patients. Many jobs for local people were provided by this hospital's existence. Around 1960 there was a staff of 450 caring for 2,737 patients with mental illness. Storthes Hall was said to be one of the largest such hospitals in Britain or indeed Europe. It closed a few years ago and has recently been converted into a student village for Huddersfield University. During the war it was used to accommodate wounded soldiers and those suffering from shellshock. They were often seen in their distinctive bright blue uniforms returning by train from Huddersfield.

During the 1930s depression, local unemployed people were set to work building sewers. Many had previously worked in the local textile industry where jobs had dwindled.'

▣ DENBYWORK ▣

'Until the 1950s there were several farms worked in the area of Upper and Lower Denby. These have gradually been eroded by residential building. Before the war there were six shops in the village – three general shops, (two being "house shops" and one being with the post office), one butcher's shop, a chip shop and a large Co-operative store, with a drapery department upstairs. There were also several travelling salesmen – greengrocer, hardware and paraffin.

Many people, in the 1920s and 1930s, worked in Denby Dale, in the textile mills. They usually walked to work. Those who lived further afield would cycle to Upper Denby, and, for a small weekly sum, would leave their bicycles at two houses at the top of the hill. They would then walk down through the woods, and collect their bikes at the top of the hill after work.

There were two small claypits in the village, employing only four or five men. There was also a monumental mason and a joiner's shop. The latter is still there.'

Working at Cockleshaw Farm, Oakworth – part of the Duke of Devonshire's estate.

'My father in law worked in a stone quarry, dressing stone for building, when he left school. There is a Roman Catholic church in Keighley (St Joseph's at Ingrow) for which he dressed nearly all the stone. We still have all his tools with his initials engraved on them. After he married he took a rented farm, in 1937, and with it he took over a milk round. He delivered from a can (again we still have it, with the ladle, and this has his name on a brass plate on the lid). His surplus milk went on the milk train which ran down the Worth Valley to Keighley at 7 am each morning calling at five villages on the way. All the farmers in the area took their full churns to the nearest station to put on the train, then a cart from the dairy in Keighley met it there to collect the milk. How busy the stations, and narrow steep roads leading to them, must have been in the early morning.

My father in law's brother worked for the local corn mill. He delivered sacks of animal feed to the farms on a horse and cart. One morning in the early 1930s he went to work as usual and was told to go to Manchester to pick up a waggon that the mill owner had bought. It seems incredible now, but he went to Manchester on the train and a mechanic there showed him how the gears worked on the waggon and he just got in and drove it home! He'd never been in a motor vehicle before – nor so far from home so it's amazing that he even found his way let alone arrived safely. It was the first waggon to be used in the village and created quite a stir.

My grandfather used to tell stories of the cattle drovers walking cows from Manchester, over the moors, to Skipton market. Grandpa said they could walk on moorland almost all the way at the turn of the century. In the summer Irish men came into the town to be hired for help with haymaking – they would live in with the family for a month.

There were three farms in the middle of the village and the farmers used to dam the beck under the bridge (where the road went over) and dip their sheep in it. What noise and mayhem there was on that day!

My father in law had seven sisters who all worked in the same mill, as weavers. The mill owners also owned the farm where they were all brought up. Their father was hot headed and had a dispute with the landlord over gathering bracken from a private wood. (This was for bedding for the cows.) He loaded his cart with bracken and went to the mill office, tipped the bracken in the doorway and then gathered all his girls together and marched them out of the mill. He took them to another half a mile away and they all started work there the same day. This tells us much of how plentiful jobs were around 1920 and also of the tenancy laws – Grandad was evicted from his farm.'

▣ AT THE ROUND HOUSE ▣

'The Round House, which stands in its own grounds in Potternewton Mount, Leeds 7, is a noticeable landmark; from the top of the house one has a very fine view of Leeds and its surroundings.

It was an old flour mill in the late 1800s which was made into living accommodation by Mr Samuel Ingham, a tall man of over six feet in height, who was married to a lady by the name of Edith, who in height barely came up to his shoulders. They were married in Adel church.

He was a joiner and undertaker and in his workshop attached to the Round House, he and two staff made coffins etc for his lucrative business.

My Father wrote the coffin plates, wooden ones for cremation and chrome ones for burial. My mother, being a French polisher by trade, used to polish the coffins. There was a lot of work put into the making of them, planed, rubbed down and highly polished. The coffins which were for burial were all lined with pitch and the ones for cremation were lined with a purple fabric.

As a child of about eight to ten years of age I took pride with the sweeping brush and swept the wood shavings from the floor for a penny a time.'

▣ BREAD AND MILK ▣

'My mother wanted to work away from Castleford, so she answered an advert in a paper requiring a girl to work in a bakery in Bradford. Mrs Pridmore went to Castleford to interview Mum and she was taken on.

Mrs Pridmore's bakery and shop was on the main road between Bradford and Leeds. She had two night bakers, working all night baking bread, teacakes, Sally Lunns and similar items. Mum lived on the premises and had to be up early to move all the baking into the shop ready for sale. Her arms used to get scratched from the crispy crusts. Another job was scrubbing the flags outside the shop: "Somebody said to me 'You'll suffer for it', when she saw me kneeling on the flags, but you don't think you will, you are tough! A grand pair of legs on me and I had nothing to kneel on. If they had just swilled the flags, there would be water everywhere, tramping into the bakery. In them days I was very strong."

"I picked up a lot of hints about baking, with only watching and suchlike, because I used to take the puff pastry which had just been made down into the cellars to 'rest' before being made up into fancy tarts. After, when the ovens had gone down and they had finished on a Saturday morning, they used to put two hams in, in separate containers, and they were left in till the men came. I do know I had to keep it at a certain temperature because I lived in."

Mrs Pridmore's mother lived with her, she did all the icing and while my mum was washing the floor she passed her a bun down. Mum didn't know what to do about it. "Get that down ye," she whispered. "Don't let them see you," and they would be walking in. One day Mum did not have time to eat the bun, so she pushed it into the bucket of water and held it down as if she was drowning somebody. She then had to replace the water.

One of the customers at the shop was the daughter of a farmer, whose property was nearby. Three sisters and three of her brothers had left home and her mother had died recently leaving her as the only woman to provide meals etc for her father and the three remaining brothers. She must have seen my mother as a useful addition to the farm, as domestic chores were not her forte. Mum was offered a place at the farm, so off she went. There was plenty of housework as well as dairy work. One brother had a milk round and one was the horse man, he broke them in and trained them. The youngest brother (my father) worked where he was needed.

To Mum the house was very large, they even had a parlour and to a coalminer's daughter this was the height of luxury. On the walls were original oil paintings with ornate gilt frames. In the kitchen they always kept three buckets by the fire, two full of coal and one full of slack to damp the fire down for the night. Their father used to sit by the fire and spit into the buckets; this upset his daughter greatly, but to the son of a woollen cloth weaver, this would be normal behaviour.

After my parents married they moved to a farm on a hill at the other side of Bradford. Mum wondered how her sister-in-law managed once she left the farm, but she had problems also. This farm did not have running water. A stream flowed along the bottom of the hill, and Mum had to work a pump handle to draw the water up the hill to the farm. Life here was very different from the streets of Castleford, healthier but lonely. Also Mum and her older sister shared their younger siblings between them once their father had died.

They also had a milk round, twice a day. Many of their customers worked in the mills, or had other jobs, so they left the money on the door step next to the jug or bowl, covered in a crochet mat with beads around the sides as a fly deterrent. Mum remarked, "I must have been strong, I had a large milk churn, a measuring jug and the reins to hold." The horse, Tommy, was a big piebald from a circus, he soon picked up the ways of the world, like all horses he soon knew the round. More importantly, he knew the houses where he would be given a biscuit. "Whoa, Tommy," but Tommy would be off rushing to the next biscuit stop.

During the heavy snowfall in March 1933, Mum still attempted to do the milk round, but under the severe weather conditions, Dad had to go with her. Often they had to clear a path for the horse to get through. The work must have been exhausting; within a few years they had moved to a farm in the centre of Ripon.'

Garforth's the milliners in 1927.

◈ IN SERVICE ◈

'My aunt was in service as an under-housemaid in 1919. She received £24 a year wages and two half days and one Sunday off per month.

The lady of the house was so fussy the coal had to be washed and bootlaces ironed.'

'I was not quite 14 in 1924 when I left home to start work. All the local girls were getting jobs in the glassworks and I wanted to do the same, but my mother would not hear of it as she did not want me working with men, who could be very coarse. Instead, my mother wrote to "her lady" for whom she had worked as a cook. My name was passed on and eventually a woman at the golf club took me on as a housemaid. There was no interview, no discussion of terms or duties – start on Monday. I discovered in the following months that my employer's expectations of a housemaid came close to matching those of my Mum's "lady" for an entire household.

My employer had four girls whom I looked after in every way. I woke them up and gave them a bath, brushed their hair and made their breakfast, before cooking breakfast for their parents. Having seen the children off to school I cleaned the house, washed, ironed and mended the clothes. In the afternoon I went shopping and ·vas instructed to buy the cheapest I could find. Then it was time to make tea, usually bread and black treacle which I ate with the children before cooking something more substantial for the parents.

Then my employers moved to the basement which enabled them to let six bedrooms. This increased my workload and I had to get up earlier and earlier as there were now more rooms to be cleaned, fires to be cleaned and laid and a bucket of coal to carry up to each room ready for the lodgers' return. They did not have any meals supplied but each evening I took them all a kettle of boiling water to make themselves a cup of tea. At night each lodger left a pair of shoes outside the door for me to polish ready for the following day.

I worked every day from getting up to going to bed and was paid six shillings a week. From this I sent home five shillings and sixpence. It cost me 1½d for a postal order and 1½d for a stamp which left only threepence a week for me which I used to save.

Once a month I had a day off to go and see my Mum. My employer lived in Swinegate from where I could catch a blue South Yorkshire bus direct to Cutsyke. The return fare was one shilling and threepence which I took out of my wages before handing over the remainder to Mum. With seven mouths to feed at home I knew that Mum would put the money to good use.

After two years in service I approached the lady of the house for a raise in wages which did not go down well and I was told I was impudent. There were four elderly ladies living at the house and I confided in one about the interview who told the others and after that every Friday they each gave me a shilling "for yourself, love".'

◨ APPRENTICE TAILOR ◨

'As I ran down the fields to catch the 7.35 workman's bus, I was trying not to get my brand new fawn patent bar shoes and white ankle socks either wet or dirty, as I must arrive at my destination looking neat and tidy. I carried a small case with my lunch and purse in, also a book in case I had any spare time to read. I was wearing a little green two-piece suit with a lovely hand-embroidered blouse, and I felt like a queen, as I had never been allowed to wear this outfit any other day than Sunday before. Where was I going?

I was on my way to my first day of work in 1941 at the age of 14. I had been apprenticed to a bespoke tailor. Being apprenticed meant I didn't receive a wage for the first six months, as I was supposed to be learning the trade. If I made progress, then at the end of the six months I would receive a wage, but no amount had been mentioned. But if my progress was not considered to be satisfactory, then there would be no wage and that would be the end of my career.

I was told my first job would be to light the stove; it was only small, but it had a large oven on top of it, where the flat irons were stacked to keep hot. The smallest of these weighed about seven pounds, and the others were much heavier. My instructions were that I might find some newspapers if I looked around, but it would be better if I brought some firewood with me in future, as they had used all they could find. Once the fire was burning I must fill it up with coke, which I would find in the cellar.

Picking up a bucket, shovel and key I made my way back down the dark stairs, through the shop, to the outside door. Behind this door was another, smaller door which led down another, even darker staircase, into a damp, horribly smelly place festooned with cobwebs which slithered over my face. I was terrified! The only light came through a small, very dirty window below street level, and I had to feel my way around, bumping my ankles on junk that must have been there for years, trying to find coke, and not knowing at all what I might pick up instead! What worried me more than anything was the thought that I was going to have to do this every day, as all the fresh water and fuel we had was down in this dreadful place, which wasn't wired for electricity.

When I arrived back in the workroom I was surprised to see all the workers sitting cross-legged on top of the tables, sewing

146

away by hand. Only the most experienced was ever allowed to use a machine. I was informed they would soon be waiting for a "hot goose" (tailors' name for a hot iron) to get on with the pressing, so I had to light the stove in a hurry. By the time I had swept the stairs and cleaned and dusted the shop, the fire was burning brightly, and the room was a little warmer. The stove was the only heating we had.

A small space was made for me on top of a table next to the boss, where, sitting cross-legged like the rest, I began to learn my trade. I was first shown how to thread a needle by holding it in the right hand and threading it with the left. This way one didn't waste a movement, as you were immediately ready to sew. The boss had many ways of saving time by movements like this.

My first tailoring job was making button-holes by hand and I practised day after day after day until the boss was satisfied they were good enough to put into trousers. I had climbed the first rung of the ladder! Next, I was given small things to press. Because the irons were always kept in the oven, the handles got very hot, so if the apprentices ever had a moment to spare they had to make iron-holders out of any spare cloth they could find. We must have used 20 such iron-holders every week, for as soon as you used them they started to scorch and burn through to your hand. I shall never forget that horrible smell of burning wool. You also had to be careful not to burn your arm on the other end of the handle. If the iron was too hot, one made a sling out of a strip of cloth threaded through the handle and dropped the whole thing into a bucket of cold water, where it spat and splashed and spurted all over the floor, with clouds of steam rising to the roof. This was a very dangerous procedure, as the water which splashed out was boiling hot, and our first-aid box contained just one tin of vaseline and a bottle of aspirins.

That first day of work was the longest day of my life! We didn't finish work until six o'clock in the evening five days a week. On Thursdays we finished at 1 pm. There were many long days to follow, but I persevered, and after six long months I received my first weekly wage – seven and sixpence. Yes, I did complete my apprenticeship, and my wage soared to the princely sum of £3 10s at the age of 21, but never got any higher.'

Barbara Gardner trained as a nurse at St James's Hospital, Leeds in the 1960s (here with a friend Vera Gunning from Dublin).

'It seemed only natural in 1940, when people in the luxury trades were being directed into the war effort, that I should choose nursing as a career, first aid having been a peace-time hobby.

The State Registered Nurse in charge of our first aid team, noting my enthusiasm, was all for me to take my full nurse training and become a state registered nurse, and strongly recommended her own training school – Manchester Royal Infirmary. Naturally "the best", which is the way all nurses think of their own training school, wherever they train.

Applications were sent for and an interview arranged. Fear on the eventful day prevents me from remembering much about the interview, but I was accepted and given a list of uniform requirements to be purchased, only from Messrs Bounds of Manchester, at the trainee's expense, and I was to present myself to be measured for same whilst in Manchester. My heart sank as the expenses mounted.

In due course the large parcel arrived by post containing: three dresses regulation length seven inches from the floor, 14 aprons, three caps, four pairs of cuffs, four Dorcas style collars later to be stiffened, pearl topped studs, one navy blue cape with red flannel lining and 50 Cash's name tapes to be stitched in specified places on each garment before being sent to the hospital laundry. This seemed a never-ending task and the first enthusiasm was slowly ebbing away, that and the feeling that Dad and the older members of the family were not so enthusiastic either about my leaving home, being the youngest and probably a bit spoilt, but I soldiered on. The aprons were stiff and hard to sew, I'd left them until the last and nearing the end, my brother came by and glancing over my shoulder said, "I wouldn't bother sewing them on too tightly, you won't stay long enough to send them to the laundry."

This must have stiffened my resolve and in September 1940 I bought a one way ticket to Manchester and I was to prove him wrong, when in 1977 I was able to look back on 37 worthwhile years in nursing.'

'I trained as an SRN from 1954 to 1958, a time when medicine was taking great leaps forward. I was at the General Infirmary in Leeds, which at that time was the more important of the two hospitals in the city and a leading medical school.

In the 1950s the Leeds General Infirmary pioneered the artificial kidney machine in the North – the only other was at Guy's Hospital in London. Patients came from all over the North and Scotland. It was huge, filling a room – now they are the size of bedside cabinets. We also had the first heart/lung machine, enabling open heart surgery to be done, and there was new treatment for tetanus – until 1954 anyone showing signs of the disease within seven days of infection was doomed.

When I started in 1954, patients were kept in bed until their stitches were removed – at that time ten days – even for fairly routine operations like appendix. We really had to *nurse* them to prevent sores and hypostatic pneumonia developing, among other things.'

▧ BOTTLED WATER ▧

'My great grandfather worked for a firm in Horsforth in the 1900s who bottled "Nethersprings Pure Horsforth Table Water" from a spring at Netherspring off Scotland Lane.'

▧ HAIRDRESSING ▧

'My sister went off to be a tailoress when she left school. But I embarked on a career as a hairdresser. About this time we moved house and went to live in a newly built house that was my parents' pride and joy and had electricity where before we used gas. We felt that this was a great improvement. I now had to travel to work on the bus by myself and felt very grown up. In the shop we wore starched white overalls and used white towels for our customers. We did trimming, bobbed and shingled hair was fashionable and marcel waving with tongs heated on a rail. Permanent waving was done by means of curlers hooked up to a monstrous looking machine. We used to set hair in rigid waves like a ploughed field and make dozens of pin curls of the ends. Christmas time was hectic when people who never came near

This mineral water delivery cart would have been a familiar sight around the Great Horton area of Bradford in the first decade of the century.

the shop at other times had to be fitted in somehow. We used to work through our dinner hour, have our tea on the run and work from 8 am until midnight attending to endless customers. I was often too tired to enjoy Christmas.

Our customers came from many walks of life and varied from the mill owners' wives and daughters to their day-girls. We also had mill girls and a cross section of all the other residents. One thing above all else you learnt was the study of human nature.'

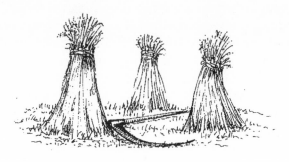

War & Peace

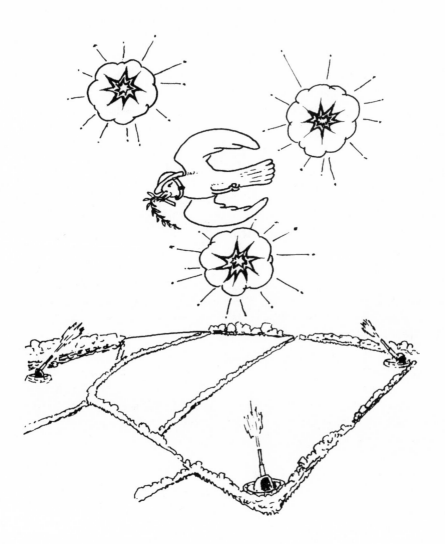

THE GREAT WAR 1914–1918

Zeppelins overhead and poor food, and the dreadful aftermath of war are remembered still by those who were children at the time.

▣ LOOKING BACK ▣

'Looking back to my young childhood days, at Purston near Pontefract, West Riding of Yorkshire, I can remember the last two or three years of the First World War. I was four years old in 1916, Dad was away somewhere fighting for his country so Mum was left alone to bring up her four children, as well as having to care for Dad's business while he was at the "front".

Mum engaged a maid to look after us. One called Violet did not like me much: I was a bit of a handful, so late one Friday winter's evening she made me wait in the entrance hall all alone in total darkness – not even gas light. I was so scared I crouched down behind a folding chair. I don't know how long I was there when I heard a rattling noise at the door. I think my hair literally stood on end as the rattling got louder and louder and then the door opened. It was Mum. What a relief – home a bit earlier. Hence the departure of Violet for good.

During night air raids we were made to sit quietly on a horsehair couch. It was terrible – not the raids exactly, although a bomb was dropped in the field at the back of the house, but the awful horsehair prickled at the back of our knees. We only had a candle lit on the table in the middle of the kitchen.'

▣ DIMMING THE LIGHTS ▣

'Things I remember – dimming the lights when the Zeppelins came over, and the dark bread we had to eat during the First World War.'

The Horsforth Home Guard in 1915.

▦ FATHER AND GRANDFATHER ▦

'Born some years after the end of the First World War, Ann remembers the effect on her father. He was lucky, his firm kept his job open, many were not so fortunate. She remembers being with him in Leeds one day when a young "old soldier" who had lost a leg and had other injuries, begged for money to buy a meal. "I won't give you money", said her father, "but I will buy you a meal, I remember what it is like to be hungry." Her father had been a prisoner of war and had also lost an eye. His discharge papers said: "No longer fit for war service".

Ann's grandfather had a son serving in France. There were very few radios in those days and the news was brought round the streets by newspaper boys who shouted "Extra, Extra" to attract attention. Grandfather posted a copy of the *Yorkshire Evening Post* to his son in France every day. One day they were sitting down for tea when son Bert suddenly walked in. He had 48 hours' leave and had come home just as he was, tired, dirty, his boots covered in mud and very hungry! Fortunately he was not one of the "Leeds Pals", a regiment raised in Leeds which suffered so many casualties – he survived.'

THE SECOND WORLD WAR 1939–1945

Just two decades later, men from West Yorkshire were again going off to war, and this time those left behind faced even greater hardship and the ever present threat from the skies. Villages and towns changed overnight with the arrival of soldiers and airmen, and we got used to sleeping in the air raid shelter and coping with rationing and shortages.

▦ THE DAY WAR BROKE OUT ▦

'I was eleven years old in September 1939, the eldest of three children – all girls. We always spent a few days before returning to school with my grandparents who lived in Marske on the Cleveland coast. Father wasn't with us on this occasion – he was training for the Civil Defence Rescue Service.

It was the journey home by coach on Sunday 3rd September that I particularly remember. It was a fine, sunny warm morning and all was well until we reached Northallerton where we stopped to buy newspapers, comics and sweets. When we got back on the coach there was obviously something the matter – some of the ladies were crying and the men were looking rather stern and uncomfortable. Then there was talk of war, which meant very little to us children.

When we arrived at Heckmondwike where we were to meet Father and get a local bus, we found that the air raid sirens were going and there was no one to meet us. Father had had to report for duty. The buses had stopped running and there was no one about at all. The only thing for us to do was to set off and walk the three miles home and most of it uphill. Mother was carrying my baby sister, and my other sister and I had to carry the luggage

A smart turnout of Coldstream Guards, who often recruited men from the Ridings. The second soldier from the right lied about his age and joined up at 16 in 1935. He sent this photo home as a postcard in 1939.

between us. Halfway up a rather steep hill we met a man coming down. He called to Mother, "You should have taken shelter", to which she replied – at the end of her tether I suppose – "I only want to get home!" '

▣ PLAIN AND SIMPLE ▣

'My memories of rationing are of going down to the village and joining a queue to get a few goodies like cake and buns, as the sugar ration did not stretch to baking our own. Our diet was plain and simple but I don't think it did anyone any harm. There was the black market, too, where people paid extra to buy coupons, and what was known as "getting it from under the counter". People in the know and with plenty of money didn't need to go short of what they wanted.'

'We were fortunate as we had an allotment and also chickens in the garden. Everything we couldn't eat fresh was jammed, pickled or bottled. "Stodge" was plentiful, and I loved scrambled eggs made from wartime dried egg. We tried whale meat, snoek, and any other gimmick which would help to vary our diet.

For quite some time Mum wore her hair tucked around a stocking top! This was a neat way of doing without a perm. Every economy was practised and I can't bear to throw anything away to this day.'

'Many things changed as the war started. Everyone began to queue for things. Most things seemed to be on ration so as soon as you saw a queue forming you joined it, then asked what they were queueing for, it didn't do to miss anything that was going. Some things were saved for special people; only expectant mothers and children under five years old could get bananas when they were available.

By the third year of the war rationing was much more severe, housewives needed to be much more resourceful to provide meals for their families. Recipe leaflets were put out by the Ministry of Food, using more obscure ingredients.

I remember ration books with coupons which could only be

KEEP THIS CARD SAFELY

NATIONAL SERVICE ACTS, 1939-1941
Certificate of Registration

Occ. Classn. No. _10-1_   Registration No. _RPH 2195_
Holder's Name _HEMINGWAY Harry_
Home Address _Old Wood Farm_
High Ardwick
Date of Birth _6-6-1904_
Holder's Signature _Harry Hemmingway_

READ THIS CAREFULLY

Care should be taken not to lose this Certificate, but in the event of loss, application for a duplicate should be made to the nearest office of the Ministry of Labour and National Service.

If you change your address, etc., you must complete the appropriate space on the other side of this certificate and post it at once. A new Certificate of Registration will then be sent to you.

If you voluntarily join H.M. Forces you should hand this certificate to the appropriate Service Officer.

You should not voluntarily give up your employment because you have been registered for military service.

This certificate must be produced on request to a constable in uniform.

A person who uses or lends this certificate or allows it to be used by any other person with intent to deceive, renders himself liable to heavy penalties.

N.S.2.

*M17527 6/41 702

J CASSERLEY

Farmers and farmworkers were exempt from the services, but had to carry a card to prove it.

exchanged for the items marked on them. If you wanted a tin of fruit you had to save up the coupons for weeks. My sister and two brothers who were all under five had green ration books and could sometimes get an occasional orange or banana. I was seven so didn't have a green ration book so could not have any, but Mam always shared any extras out between the four of us. I remember queueing at the local sweetshop for my Grandad's week's sweet ration, two ounces of Poor Bens. There was always an extra one for me as my "wages".

The blackout was very hard, going to work in the winter mornings when there was no moon was difficult, you had to feel your way along the wall and hope you ended up in the right place. Between our house and my Grandma and Grandad's house there were railings along the side of the canal, so Grandad always went home by "rail", feeling his way along the railings. There were 193 rails before he had to turn right into their street, and they lived at the fourth lamp post down the street. I don't know what he would have done if they had removed the railings

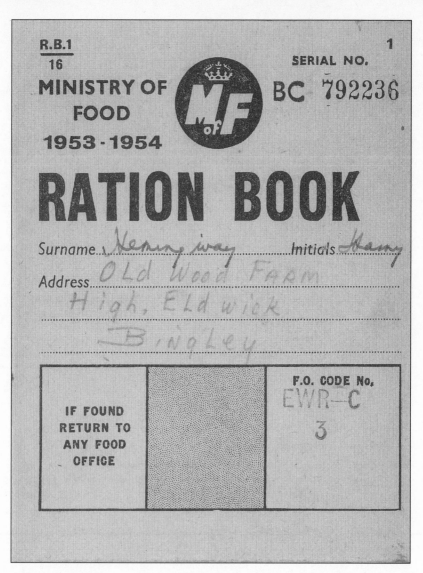

R.B.1

16

MINISTRY OF FOOD

1953-1954

SERIAL NO.

BC 792236

RATION BOOK

Surname. Hemingway .... Initials Harry

Address. Old Wood Farm
High, Eldwick
Bingley

IF FOUND
RETURN TO
ANY FOOD
OFFICE

F.O. CODE No.
EWR—C
3

Ration books became a part of life and continued to be issued until well into the 1950s.

for the war effort like they did at the local houses, schools and parks.

Everyone had to black out their windows and heaven help

A wedding group from 1943. Every effort was made to make the day special.

anyone who showed a light, a great bellow of "Turn off that light" could be heard in the street if even a tiny chink of light was showing. You had to take a torch out with you, which had tape across the end so only a small slit of light showed through, car headlights had to be taped up the same and always dipped.'

'My father made covers for the small window above the door out of wood, but he left a small hole in the middle to enable it to be removed in daytime and I remember the warden knocking on the door to say that there was a chink of light shining through, so after that we had a cork made to fit the hole and this was put in every night.

I also remember my uncle, who lived at the far side of Bradford had a car and because of the blackout, every so far he used to get out to find where he was. I think he only had the car because of some work he was doing.

I was a bridesmaid during the war and the whole family saved coupons to provide the food for the wedding feast and my mother obtained coupons from a large family to buy velvet to make my dress, but there was not enough for undies so she cut up some lace curtains to trim my knickers. I vividly remember being very uncomfortable with itchy legs.

When I went to the grammar school sweets were still on ration and we used to eat Oxo cubes, dried bananas and anything we could find. I had an aunt in Canada and she sent the family parcels which contained cream cheese and lovely red apples which we spread out in the attic to save them as long as possible. The parcels were wrapped in flour sacks and sewn up; when they were opened the material was used to make pillow cases and tablecloths, which my mother embroidered and I think they looked very nice.'

◙ UNACCUSTOMED TASKS ◙

'When the war came things were very different and we all found ourselves doing unaccustomed tasks. I eventually left my hairdressing and went off to work with a radar team, a very secret business, and a very different scenario to the one that I was used to. People moved up from the south of England who seemed to believe that we should all still be wearing clogs and shawls.

It was a good thing if you had a reasonable wardrobe at the start of the war as most things began to get scarce. As coupons were introduced people became very ingenious. Lots of curtain material (unrationed) dresses began to appear, brightly coloured shoelaces cheered up worn shoes. High heels became a thing of the past and underwear could be made out of parachute silk. I learnt how to pick up ladders in stockings with a tiny hook, a great saving. Everyone walked about in white riding macs which suddenly became easy to obtain. Pyjama jackets became a good substitute for blouses when coupons were in short supply, and it became fashionable to wear collars turned out over jackets. We found it easier to go to work wearing trousers and a new fashion in trouser suits began.

It was possible to obtain make-up if you heard when stocks

came into the local chemist's shop and if you could get there in time, usually brandishing a pound note, willing to take whatever was on offer even if it was not your usual brand.

Leg make-up instead of the not very nice stockings was the thing to wear, in summer anyway. When we worked overtime, as we often did, we used to stay for tea when there would be a nice line in shepherd's pie and something called Spam, which we had not heard of before but which was, and I think still is, very tasty. It would arrive served up with chips and beetroot, one of the meals I remember in wartime. We used to have ENSA concerts in the canteen at lunch time.'

▣ IN THE PARK ▣

'Air raid shelters were built on Armley Park during the war but only once did I ever go across to them during a raid, with my parents. I recall running across the park and looking up at the sky, brightly lit with flares, flashes and incendiary bombs falling. My father worked at Greenwoods & Batleys, on munitions, during the war years, and often came home with cigarette lighters and other ornaments made from bullets. These adorned our sideboard for years!'

▣ BOMBS BY THE ROAD ▣

'During the war bombshells were stacked on the sides of many minor roads by the American forces who were stationed at Scout Dyke Camp near Penistone. Until this time the roads had just been dirt tracks but the Americans built them properly before use. The soldiers lived in wooden huts, which had originally been put up for the navvies who built Scout Dyke Reservoir. The bombs came and went continually – where to we never knew because we had been taught that "careless talk costs lives".'

▣ STRIPES ON THE LAMP POSTS ▣

'When the war started the lamp posts were painted with white stripes so that we could see them in the blackout.'

Irene Broadfield in 1942 – we still managed to look glamorous, despite rationing and shortages.

▨ War in the Village ▨

'During the war when everyone was urged to "dig for victory", an Allotments Association was founded in Stocksmoor village. It became a thriving organisation with meetings held in the local pub and an annual show. When soldiers were billeted at Kirkburton, they loaned a big marquee to the association for the annual show. One year this was erected behind the Clothiers Arms and a dance floor was put down for entertainment in the evening.

When German bombers flew to bomb Sheffield their route lay over the village of Stocksmoor and I remember one night when only Mother and I were at home, we were terrified as we sat in the dark listening to the pieces of anti-aircraft shells rattling on the farm roof.

Stocksmoor was surrounded by signalling posts during the war. I used to go on the train to Shepley where the Army put on a dance and provided the band.

After the bonfire on VE Day the men of the village got talking in the Clothiers Arms over a celebratory pint. They decided that what the village needed was a village hall and a fund was started that night. It was 28 years later before their dreams were realised and a purpose-built hall became a reality.'

▨ In the Gloom ▨

'In the late summer of 1943 I was granted leave from my unit in southern England and after a long and tedious rail journey through the southern counties, then across London to Kings Cross, I finally arrived, unexpected, at home just as daylight was fading.

In those days doors were seldom, if ever, locked and I dashed up the path, through the back door and there, in the gloom inside the kitchen (the lights had not been switched on because of blackout regulations) I espied at the table a figure breathing in grunts and hisses and who spoke in an unrecognisable voice, yet the figure had obviously recognised me.

It transpired that my mother was at her government directed war work and my father was providing a variation to the

165

stringent food rationing by peeling onions (unrationed). To prevent him "crying" he had donned his wartime issue gas mask and this proved most effective for the purpose, but the sight of this faceless person in the gloom and the muffled distorted voice emanating from the gas mask scared the living daylights out of me and I was ready to drop my kit bag and make a run for it!

The situation ended in uncontrollable laughter and caused many a smile in later years.'

◙ A Secret Visit! ◙

'George VI, and the Royal Family visited Pool in Wharfedale in March 1944. Like so many war time events this was not to be generally known, but as today there is always a leak! My father at that time was a Special Constable, required to be on duty this day. Hence he told me to tell my friends to be around the bridge in Pool about 10.30 am, walking the dog!

Sure enough, quite a number of Pool residents assembled near the bridge, the children came out of the nearby school and we all waited – for what? We did not know.

However, soon we could hear faint, and then louder, cheering. A big car came, which pulled up the Harrogate side of the bridge. The Royals got out, climbed the stile into a muddy field, and went to view a rope gadget which the Royal Engineers had made for getting kit over a river or ravine. On returning to the car the party drove slowly past us all giving a wave and a cheer, receiving a smile and royal wave in return then away they went to AVRO. Only the two local swans flew up river by way of royal salute.

What I best recall is the hearty cheers of those men from the Tank Corps who were stationed along Leathley Lane.'

◙ Strangers in the Village ◙

'During the war I lived in a village, Scarcroft, which is about seven miles from Leeds. A family of five – a mother, her sister, and three children – came to live in a house there. They were from the East End of London and were known throughout the village as the 'vacuees. Two of the children came to school and they found it hard to come to terms with country life. They pined for the pavements and hustle and bustle of London and we, in turn, found it difficult to understand their sharp cockney wit and strange accent. As soon as it was safe to do so, they returned to London – they couldn't wait to get back – and the village missed the cockney greetings cheerfully flung at all and sundry.

We also had a "Displaced Persons" camp in the village during the war. The men came mainly from Poland and were quite a cheerful crowd. Some of them worked on local farms and were regarded with respect by the locals, unlike the Italian prisoners of war who were regarded as a lazy lot! The Poles integrated well into village life. They went to the local dances and gave concerts at their camp to which they invited the locals. The jokes were lost on the English audience of course, as they could not understand a word of what was said, but there was some excellent singing and dancing. After the war they all left to return from whence they came, and who knows what they went back to.

At this time too we had a murder in the village. Old Miss Barker was found battered to death in her cottage. She was always called "old", but probably wasn't much more than middle-aged. Eccentric she certainly was! She was always dressed in the fashion of the last century – long skirt, high-necked blouse, long coat, buttoned boots, and atop her neat head would be a hat with a large feather. She was quite small, ramrod straight, and always walked briskly. There was no apparent motive for her murder and her killer was never found. As children we would hurry past her rose-covered cottage, scared we might see her ghost!'

❖ IT WAS BAD ❖

'I was eleven years old when war broke out in 1939. There were no lights at all outside, with thick black curtains at every window and over the door. A piece of string went from the door to the light, and when the door was opened a shade came down over the light made of a kind of cardboard, so that no rays of light escaped outside. When the air raid siren sounded we went

57 Ordsall Road
Retford.
5th Sep.1939

Dear Mummy Daddy + Stitcher

Thank you very much for the letter I was so excited to get it. ~~Bess~~ Bessie got one too and her friend Sylvia who is staying at Mrs Browns. Auntie has a friend called Mr ~~Estton~~ Eston who takes us Blackburying + we get eversomany for Auntie but the worst of it is that we have to take our gasmasks with us. Did you hear the sirrans? Auntie did but did not wake us. How are Stitcher and Nelson Dash and Mac? There is a doggie called Patsy next door. I will write again soon will you too please?

XXXXX XXXXXXX Love to all give my love to Tony W Shirley

A letter home to 'Mummy and Daddy', written by a young evacuee from the West Riding who had been sent to stay with an aunt in Nottinghamshire.

under the stone stairs in the kitchen. Mum sat with my six year old brother on her knee, and I sat on a small stool. Dad had to leave us, as he was an air raid warden and had a job to do outside. I was very frightened and used to push my fingers into my ears to deaden the sound of the falling bombs and the big guns on the ground. When the all clear went my ears ached and my fingers were quite numb.

It was bad in the Dewsbury area in 1940. An incendiary bomb fell on Chickenley Sunday school, completely destroying it. We had only left a few hours before, having set out all the stalls for our Christmas sale of work. The next day I went with my father to see the damage, and there was nothing left but charred timbers. I found one old penny, all that remained from the many weeks' hard work making things for the stalls.

The weaving shed of Syke Ing Mills, belonging to Thomas & David Lee, had a direct hit with a bomb, and I can remember watching it blaze. Another bomb fell on Wakefield Road, Dewsbury. It made a huge crater and destroyed some cottages. My friend lived next door, and their house was still standing. We could hear the enemy planes going overhead when they bombed Sheffield, and I can remember seeing Ossett church silhouetted against the bright red sky. The soldiers had guns and searchlights at Caulms Wood. At that time, 1942 to 1943, there were no buses, and the soldiers brought their army lorries on to the bus route to pick us up and take us to school in Dewsbury.

Later on, when I was working near Dewsbury station, trains used to bring Italian prisoners of war at 8.30 in the morning. They went off towards the old Feast Ground to work and returned at tea time, always giving us a wave, and sometimes picking up odd flowers that had been dropped around the market and throwing them to us as they passed.

Until the outbreak of war, our annual holiday was one week in July, known as Dewsbury Feast week. The Monday of the previous week all our holiday clothes were packed into a huge trunk, which was sent on in advance to our landlady's address. On the following Saturday we caught the steam train from Dewsbury to Leeds, and changed there to a train for Redcar. We always went to the same place year after year, but we loved it. Most people stayed with a family in those days. The landlady did all the cooking, but we did our own shopping, taking in whatever we wanted for dinner; it was called "keeping yourself". If the landlady had an allotment you could buy potatoes and vegetables from her. At the end of the week, when she gave you the bill for the rooms, there was always an item "For the Cruet" – the use of salt, pepper and vinegar. This always made us laugh.

During the war we spent our holidays at home, sometimes going by bus to Leeds, then on to Ilkley or Otley, calling for our lunch at the Civic Centre, then going down to the river and into the open-air swimming baths. Our first holiday after the war we went again to Redcar. Part of the beach had been cleared for the holidaymakers, but there were still great concrete blocks and rolls of barbed wire scattered about.'

▣ CONVOYS ON THE RING ROAD ▣

'One thing that had to stop in September 1939 was the building of the Leeds ring road. But a good part of it was already completed, including the part next to my family home. Oh! those wonderful wide grass verges, where it seemed to be always sunny, and we youngsters would play endless games in large groups from dawn to dusk.

Red letter days of excitement were provided by the large convoys which would often pass through on the ring road, with all the troops moving around the country. There would be literally hundreds of vehicles to each convoy, sometimes taking most of the day to pass; there would be tanks, lorries, armoured cars, jeeps, all filled with soldiers of many allied nations besides our own lads, also prisoners of war from Germany and Italy.

There were constant long stops, while each section waited for others to catch up. We children would gather round chatting to the troops, trying to converse with the foreigners, and exchanging the few sweets then available.

These convoy sections were kept in contact (without today's walkie-talkies!) by to-ing and fro-ing motorcycle despatch riders – these were our great heroes. I remember for years thinking that the most romantic job in the world would be that of a despatch rider, war or no!'

▣ 'ARRY'S ATTACHE CASE ▣

'Our Anderson shelter faced that of our neighbours. The most amusing thing was that the family (who hailed from the Holmfirth area originally) had a mysterious attache case. We had many a laugh when the wife used to shout, " 'Arry! 'as tha gotten t'atchie case wi' thee?" She was more concerned about that than 'Arry's steel helmet or gas mask.

As we lived on a farm, the shelters had been sunk into a copse, the trees providing camouflage (a thing drilled into us time and again by the ARP wardens). Our friends had to come the full length of the long copse, in the blackout.

One night, Harry fell over a tree root – hurting his ankle – but all his wife could shout was, "Pick thissen up 'Arry, an' whatever tha does, doan't loise t'atchie." Anyone would have thought it contained the Crown Jewels.

Poor old Harry groped around in the darkness, not daring to use a torch for fear of the warden shouting "Put that light out", so he had to depend upon the odd flicker as searchlights scanned the skies. Shrapnel all around him (from the guns at Post Hill) Harry looked for his belongings, in sheer desperation.

Mrs Harry used to drink distilled water, which had been tightly sealed in screw top pop bottles. (It was supposed to be "in case of emergency" along with those horrible ship biscuits – in the event of our being trapped without food or water). Harry's wife acquired a taste for this water and today one would have said she was "hooked" on it. The night Harry lost the little brown attache case, she drank cupfuls of the stuff, as if it was a tranquilising potion.

Eventually, Harry stumbled into the shelter to be met by a string of abuse from his wife for having retrieved his gas mask, even the 'tatchie, but the mysterious contents were missing (it having burst open on hitting the ground). We had never known what it contained but as the all clear sounded, a full scale search was mounted by one and all. I found the documents – no wonder his missus carried on – they were insurance policies which she had taken out on 'Arry!

To the best of my knowledge, she hasn't required them all these years later but I often wonder if they are in another 'tatchie and if she keeps the new key fastened to her corsets.'

A Child's War

For some children the war brought excitement, for many it brought fear, but it became a part of our lives and we came to accept its oddities and inconveniences.

◙ WARTIME BATHNIGHT ◙

'As many will remember, during the war we were only allowed three or four inches of water in the bath. To ensure you only used this amount a line was painted inside the bath at the appropriate level. Families used to get over this by bathing the children first and adding a further few inches for each person taking a bath. Guess who had the most water, yes! of course, it was the man of the house.

I used to hate this and would prefer to have an all over wash or a "bath" in the lovely big kitchen sink as I could have the water deeper, so I used to ensure that I had a bath every night in the sink by getting as dirty as possible whilst out playing. The sighs and tut-tuts of "When will you remember you are a little girl and not a street urchin?", were just like water off a duck's back to me as I knew I would have a "bath" with plenty of water and time to mess about without the usual, "Hurry up, the water will be cold".'

◙ TOO YOUNG TO UNDERSTAND ◙

'In 1939, at the beginning of my second year at Notre Dame we were evacuated to Boston Spa. We had a brown carrier bag each with a tin of corned beef and other emergency rations. We stood in the village hall, with our luggage, our luggage labels and our gas marks until we were claimed. I was billeted with a very well-to-do family, an elderly lady and her unmarried daughter. They were very "County". They lived in a beautiful house in huge grounds, and had three maids, a gardener and a chauffeur. They also had two cars, I think the big one was a Rolls, and two Kerry Blue dogs. We had our own play room, bedroom and bathroom, and every evening Mrs Clough or Miss Barbara (as we called her), would come and play cards or pencil and paper games with us, until supper was brought in, a huge jug of milk, fruit and biscuits. And every night one of them came to tuck us up and give us a goodnight kiss. I was only there for three months, but they couldn't have been kinder, and I kept in touch with them until they died.

When I came back home to Leeds a large table was installed in our small living room. This was an indoor air raid shelter. It had a mattress and I can remember sometimes being allowed to sleep down there, and I used to listen (illicitly) to Vera Lynn's late night programme, and get all sentimental when she crooned such tear-jerkers as *I Haven't Said Thanks for that Lovely Weekend*. Hearing the air raid sirens in the distance, gradually coming nearer, and seeing the searchlights criss-crossing the sky, hearing the heavy drone of planes, and thinking, "Is it one of theirs?" was exciting. I was too young really to understand the horror of war. I remember the neighbours having stirrup pump practices, and the letters ARP painted on Mr Greenberg's wall, he was the chief of our home protectors! My uncle Tom, who lived across the road, was in the police. Every time there was a night air raid he had to walk a couple of miles to the police station, blowing his whistle. When the all clear sounded he would walk home, ringing a bell. I remember him coming into the house ringing his bell and calling out, "Hot pies and peas." Sometimes he wouldn't even have time for a cup of tea, he would have to set off again immediately for the police station.

One evening an incendiary bomb fell in the grounds of Notre Dame, and it was put out by Sister Theresa, who became a school heroine from that day forward. At school we had our adopted ship, the *Nelson*. We wrote to the sailors, knitted socks, mittens and balaclavas for them, and had *Nelson* Days when we arranged all sorts of activities to raise money for other goodies to send to "our" sailors.

Even in wartime 4th November was still Plot Night, or Mischievous Night, and even if we weren't allowed bonfires on the following night, we still prevailed upon our Mums to let us go out as soon as it got dark, just for a few minutes. Our "mischief" consisted of knocking on doors then running away, removing dustbin lids, or equally innocuous acts, all within the safety of the two or three streets around. There were no holidays for us, my father died in January 1941, but there used to be Holiday at Home Week, when there would be all sorts of activities, in local parks, such as "scavenger hunts". I remember after the war, when the famous Woodhouse Feast came to Leeds. It was the mecca for all young people, and one could go there in safety, no gangs or violence. Yes, I grew up in a different world.'

▨ A City Child's War ▨

'The war affected us all when the air raids started. Living in an industrial part of Leeds with a power station in the valley, flanked by the railway, river and canal, we had day and night time raids. At night my brother and I sat under the stone cellar steps as this was supposed to be the safest part of the house. The cellar window was frosted, but we could see the flashes as the bombs were dropped and of course we heard them. I'd call to my Mum asking if the bombs were getting nearer, she'd be watching out from the front door. Thank goodness we never were hit. One of my pals whose home didn't have a cellar had to go to the air raid shelter, and she had a siren suit to put over her nightie. I was really envious of that siren suit, I was wrapped in a blanket.

Air raid shelters were everywhere, also large water tanks to fight a blaze. These were uncovered to save time, and although there was a danger of children climbing into them I don't remember them being covered.

In the infants' department of our school when there was an air raid, depending on which class we were in, we either went to the air raid shelter in the playground, or to a windowless store room at the side of the infants' building. (I hated the stuffed parrot in a cage!). The air raid shelter in the playground had no doors or windows, it was like a maze with rooms and an open entrance at the top and the bottom ends. It was oblong shaped with a concrete roof. There was no light so torches were used, but we children knew our way through by touch.

Books were not printed so it was common to have one reading or reference book between three children. Paper was not to be wasted. No lines missed between sums, and if you made a blot it meant a smack from the headmistress. We had free milk, and also took our own spoon so we could have a daily dose of malt and cod liver oil.

After an air raid the destruction was to be seen. Rows of terraced houses with gaps of one or more houses missing, these had been homes of friends sometimes. I don't remember if anyone died in these bombings, but they must have, or been severely injured. If they survived they'd lost everything.

Living where we did it was a miracle we were never hit, but as soon as the power station received news of bombers heading our way they would send up a smoke screen which more than covered that part of the valley. I was lucky as nobody in my family was killed in the war. I do remember the sadness when our neighbour's son was killed as he parachuted from his plane. His girlfriend was pregnant so my Mum gave her my outgrown cot.

I went to Burley Methodist Sunday school with all my pals. Mum went to bed on Sunday afternoons after doing the washing on Sunday morning. Dad usually went for a game of bowls to Burley Park in the summer, and for a game of snooker at the bowling club in winter.

Nobody moved house in wartime. If a house became empty it was usually because someone had died. This happened in my cousin's street, so she put in a bid and was successful, and so had a home for when her husband came home after the war, but she stayed at her Mum's until then. Furniture was in short supply, too. Items were handed down, borrowed, bought secondhand or rented.

It was a close community during the war. My mum knew everyone in our street and some round about. If you wanted a word with a neighbour all you had to do was knock on the adjoining wall, and sometimes a coded knock meant "come in for a cup of tea". We shared good news as well as bad tidings.

Some young women whose husbands were away in the forces

went to town a lot to the pubs, and had men friends so Mum would say they were shameful and "no better than they should be". I couldn't understand that! Anyone with a funny name our gang thought was German. Unfortunately, when President Roosevelt died we thought he was German and cheered. We were soon put right. We also thought the Germans doing the goose-step was a funny dance whilst they invaded our allies. We didn't understand.

At the time I didn't feel deprived by the conditions we lived in during the war. I, like all my friends, didn't know any better. We were loved and cared for by our parents and families, and they did their best for us. I know that after every raid a general sigh of relief went up when we hadn't been bombed – this time anyway. As the saying goes – we just had to get on with it, and that's what everyone did!'

◼ CUSHIONS ON OUR HEADS ◼

'Born three years before the start of the war, I was too young to remember the horror of war, but I do have memories of events, places and people from my childhood. Living in Leeds, near heavy industry, there were some air raids on the local area. Mum, a widow, took my brother, Alec, and I to the next door neighbour's and we children sat under a stout wooden table with cushions on our heads while the adults drank tea and chatted.

I only saw one enemy plane. It happened when Mum and I were talking to the air raid warden. We thought the local park was on fire, but as the blaze got closer and larger we lay on the ground as we realized it was a German plane on fire. (I later heard that it crashed somewhere near Adel.)

School was Queen's Road Primary – a Victorian building with high ceilings and large rooms, (and outside toilets – we tried not to "go" in winter). There was an air raid shelter in the yard, but it was so dark and spooky I think we would rather have faced the bombs than spend any length of time in there.

As Mum had to go to work, Alec and I had three meals a day at school – breakfast and tea were bread and jam with cocoa, the hot midday meal came in large metal drums. Our "dining room" was the infants' hall and we had to help with tables and clearing away. Our school collected old newspapers (we were told, to build planes with) and jam jars which were sold for school funds. We had a lovely flower garden that we were taught to take care of, but it had to go when the railings were needed for the "war effort".'

▣ ALL THE EXCITEMENT ▣

'During the war, in the evenings we would go next door, my Mum and I, taking our knitting, while my Dad and our next door neighbour were out fire watching. We always listened to the wireless. Our favourite programmes were *Dick Barton, Special Agent*, and *Paul Temple*. We'd spend hours, our needles clicking, discussing "who dun it"?

I remember being kept in at school, when the sirens went and the teacher sent me home. I had to run through three fields, and I could hear the aeroplanes overhead. I was so scared, and never had I been so glad to stumble into my house, gasping for breath and shaking with fright.

Soon after that, I tried to get away from it all, dressed in my Mum's high heeled shoes and her best dress, pushing my doll's pram. I was halfway to Halifax (I lived in Elland) when a very bemused milkman found me, and brought me home in his horse and cart.

If the sirens went we would go into the pantry, though what good it would have been if a bomb should have hit us, I shall never know. The nearest we got to danger was when a V2 bomb dropped a few hundred yards from our home. To my annoyance I missed all the fun and excitement as I slept soundly through it all. I think my Mum was glad I didn't waken up till it was all over.'

▣ WE STILL HAD HOLIDAYS ▣

'I was ten years old when the war broke out. I remember arriving home from Sunday school and hearing the news, but it did not mean much to me at the time. I was at the point of changing schools and we did not start on the day planned and then went alternate days and even Saturday mornings for a short time. Then things seemed to settle down.

I do not ever remember being hungry and as my father kept hens we always had plenty of fresh eggs. Although his hens were only a hobby (he worked full-time in a munitions factory) he had his regular customers and had to deal with their ration books.

My father loved his holidays and even during the war we went on holiday – travelling in very overcrowded trains to the nearest seaside resort. Needless to say, we always took a supply of fresh eggs in addition to our clothes. In those days we stayed in modest boarding houses – providing the landlady with food coupons and our own eggs, enough for the week. Much to my parents' disgust we did not always get eggs for breakfast but no doubt the landlady enjoyed her breakfast.

When I was 14 I joined the GTC (Girls Training Corps). We wore forage caps, white blouse and navy skirt if we had them. We attended once a week and did drills, marching, were taught Morse Code and had outdoor sports activities. My father was rather worried about me joining the GTC because he was convinced I would be "called up" much sooner than 18 years of age because of it. I do remember going on parade in town.

We did not suffer much from bombs in our area but often had air raid warnings. I would be wakened and taken downstairs to spend the rest of the time until the all clear went, sitting in a deck chair under the stairs. We did not have an air raid shelter as next door had a cellar and in a real emergency we were expected to use their cellar.'

▨ AT SCHOOL ▨

'Air raid shelters were built in the school grounds and a practice evacuation was held from time to time. These were quite enjoyable as they made a diversion from lessons. For the first few months of the war we had to carry our coat and gas mask around the classrooms all day. We collected "bun" pennies for War Weapons Week. (These were the ones which showed Queen Victoria with her hair worn in a bun.) We also collected bus tickets and silver paper for salvage. We all knitted scarves, gloves and balaclavas for the crew of the school's adopted ship, which was an oil tanker. I remember the captain once paid a visit and spoke to the assembled school. Visits to the swimming baths were cancelled (hence I still can't swim). Soldiers billeted near the school used our hockey pitch and churned up the turf. Clothing was on coupons but school uniform survived, with a good trade in secondhand garments.'

▣ OUR PARTY ▣

'I was born in a street very similar to Coronation Street except that we had a lovely slope down to the bottom, which was used by all the local children on crisp winter evenings to "sledge". The track was like glass until Mrs Stubbs, a neighbour without children, used to throw all the ashes from the fire across the road, but we were never deterred for long. At the top of the street was the school which was on the main road and a chemist's and, my haven of paradise, the Futurist cinema. We had three cinemas in the district and they changed films twice a week so if you were lucky or had tenpence you could see six films and I managed it on more than one occasion.

Just off the street in a field was the Mission, our place of worship, or rather the place to learn to smoke and swap cigarette cards. It was here that Mrs Warren, who ran the Mission, told us about Sidney Speight being taken prisoner by the Japanese; fortunately he came home and we had a party and put flags all across the street. I expected to see someone who looked like Walter Pidgeon, but Sid was small and bald and just ordinary. We had wonderful Anniversaries at the Mission when we got to sing or say a poem and receive a prize for good attendance. All the children had a new outfit for Whitsuntide and after the anniversary was the Whitsuntide Walk when we could show off the best Barnsley British Co-op could offer. After the war a girl in the street called Sheila who was very "modern" wore the New Look and I remember watching her walk out on Sunday with her young man in this suit with a long skirt and a frill round the bottom of the jacket. We kids thought she looked silly, but we all tried to dress up like her when we were playing in the backyard, pressing petals to make perfume and wearing lace curtains for a veil.

When VE Day approached the men in the street formed a committee to collect money for a street party. My Dad was the treasurer and he took my mother's only prized possession which was a suede, silk-lined jewellery box (this had been given to her by a lady when my Mum was in service) to collect the money in. Well, you can imagine what happened to it. She still has it, the silk is split and the suede is shiny, but it reminds me of all those years ago every time I see it, of the sad times and the happy times.

When the party day arrived and the fireworks had been bought, the trestle tables from the pub were put up in the field at the back of our house, all the sandwiches were set out and the pop and crisps, everything was ready. Sonny Wass who was in charge of the fireworks, whilst waiting for darkness, decided to have a smoke. Yes, you guessed it, he threw the match away, straight into the fireworks and for two minutes we had the most exciting, fantastic display you have ever seen.'

◙ ODD THINGS ◙

'During the war when I was about seven years old, one Saturday I went with my mother to the market in town where we made some careful purchases (both money and food were in short supply). On returning to the bus station we decided to go into the ladies – we must have both gone into the same cubicle. We pulled the chain and turned to open the door and a cabbage rolled off Mum's basket and fell down the toilet. We both looked in horror but knew we could not afford to leave it so Mum fished it out, much to my amusement, and we went home.

I was threatened not to tell my father what had happened but I remember having a fit of the giggles at Sunday dinner time. I don't know if we ever told Dad the full story but I do know that he took an allotment and grew wonderful vegetables for us for the duration of the war and after.

In the early war years before everyone had an air raid shelter we had to share with a neighbour. We had a lovely black spaniel called Jet and one day when the sirens went we could not find him. We eventually located him in the shelter next door but one. He always had the sense to go there immediately the sirens sounded.

I also remember waking up in my father's arms wrapped in a blanket on the way to the same air raid shelter during an alert. It was a very odd feeling to wake up in the middle of the street!'

THE EVACUEES

Even before war became official, children left their homes in the cities to find safer accommodation. Many returned home after a while, but some stayed away for the duration of the war. It was a difficult time, both for parents and children – and for the hosts who took them in.

▨ ON THE FARM ▨

'On Sunday, 3rd September 1939 when war was declared, I was already evacuated on to a farm two miles from Harewood village. As a ten year old from the centre of Leeds, I had no idea what war meant. I think I expected planes and bombs to come swooping out of the sky immediately. Instead, 1 looked around me and saw the green fields sloping down to the river, the birds singing, the cows gently cropping the grass, and hens scratching in the dust of the farmyard. If this was war, it was more peaceful than anything I had ever experienced.

Although the farm was part of the Harewood Estate, it had no electricity, gas, water or sewerage. We drew water from the pump, and on Friday nights seven of us shared the same bath water, heated in the copper in the washhouse.

We used oil lamps, and went to bed by candlelight. I learned to

181

milk the cows by hand, and had my first lesson in reproduction when I saw a litter of pigs born. Haymaking was done by hand, and I was allowed to ride on the cart horse as it brought the hay in.

The following year the Leeds schools opened again and with regret I left the little village school and returned to the Victorian building with 600 pupils – back to playing in the streets, with the trams rattling past, and no more warm milk, fresh eggs, and butter.'

◼ BILLETED IN TADCASTER ◼

' "The day war broke out" I was safely and happily billeted with a young, newly-married couple in Tadcaster. The girls of West Leeds High School had left Armley two days previously, on buses, not knowing what to expect.

I vividly remember standing in the hall at Tadcaster grammar school, being issued with a brown paper carrier bag of provisions which included a packet of cream crackers, and waiting to be claimed by someone who was going to look after me. I was lucky!

We had to share the school building with its rightful occupants, so they used it in the morning and we took it over for the afternoons. Our mornings had to be filled, and our teachers must have had to think hard about what to do with us. I was part of the youngest form and there were only four of us, I think, so we were taken on "nature walks", for which I have always been grateful to Miss Padman, a terrifying lady from Boston Spa, who helped me to appreciate not only English literature but also the beauties and wonders of the countryside.

By Christmas we had returned home, but after more than 50 years I still remember music lessons in the church hall, the smell of the maltings and the breweries, the sight of a sunlit spider's web decorated by melting frost, blackberrying on a local farm, singsongs at school to cheer us up on Friday afternoons, and a visit to the smithy at Stutton, about which I wrote my first contribution to the school magazine, but, above all, the kindness I received from my hosts and their relations and friends.'

◙ REMOVED TO THE PENNINES ◙

'Around 1940 when the war had just started, it was decided that my sister and I should be removed from the hazards of city life in Leeds. As my maternal grandparents had originated from the high Pennine village of Heptonstall this was to become our home for the duration of hostilities. We resided briefly with relatives in Mytholmroyd and Hebden Bridge before renting a cottage at Slack Bottom, Heptonstall. Although small, this house had the luxury of an inside toilet but the great attraction for me was our neighbour Jim-A-Nancy's, well known locally for carrying a ferret in his coat pocket. This gentleman made a billet stick for me and taught me to play the game – a form of knur & spell.

There were many characters in the village; I remember Mr Moseby of Fields Farm who told me he had seen the ghost of a lady walk straight through the barn wall; "Shiney", so called because of the state of the seat of his trousers; Mr Thomas, our milkman, who had to walk on the top of walls to deliver milk in thick snow. We picked docks and made dock pudding boiled with young nettles and onions and thickened with oatmeal; it is a local delicacy eaten with bacon and eggs and quite delicious. My grandfather had been a hill farmer and something of a landowner, he had been known as Jack of Benthead – although the farm known as Benthead was a total ruin at that time. I still return to Heptonstall to revive old memories and to visit my grandparents' grave in Heptonstall churchyard looking out over Eves towards Stoodley Pike. A timeless, unchanging view in this ever changing world.'

◙ SEEING MY FATHER CRY ◙

'I remember being evacuated to Lincoln at the age of six. Seeing my father cry for the first time as we congregated in the playground at Armley Park school will always remain in my memory. I was with my cousin, and most of the school, including teachers and headmistress – all carrying our gas masks, of course, and wondering what homes we were going to be sent to. I was too young to be concerned – I thought I was going on my holidays! My cousin, Barbara, and I were well cared for in

Lincoln but everyone drifted home again after several weeks, although some stayed longer.

My aunt and uncle who had a farm at Pateley Bridge sent for me to go live there with my six cousins to escape the bombing. I was there for a year and went to the village school. On Friday nights (Amami night, as we called it – referring to Amami shampoo) we were all bathed one at a time in front of the fire in a large wooden peggy tub. I was always first in when the water was clean, because I was the visitor!

I remember sleeping on a camp bed in our cellar which had been reinforced with steel girders; sandbags outside every house – some of them often leaked sand – helped along by tiny fingers; men coming to cut off our railings and being quite heartbroken when they took the park railings and bandstand away "for the war effort"; a boy swallowing a bullet in my class and being rushed off to Leeds Dispensary.

We had lots of air-raid practices at school. After the register had been taken, and milk money collected, we had to line up and follow the teacher to the school shelter. Gas masks were checked by ARP men and sometimes we had to sit through a whole lesson with our gas masks on – to get used to them. I never did. They smelt horrid and the boys used to blow in them and make rude noises.

No 14 was my tram into Leeds City Square. I would get off there with my mother just so that we could walk past Trinity church and see the little deformed man who sat outside the church begging. He was nearly always there. Woodbine Lizzie was another famous Leeds character in the war years, and after.

As a child my outings were usually to Roundhay Park or Temple Newsam. There was always a crowd of us, aunts, uncles and friends and it took for ever getting there on the trams. We nearly always seemed to have tomato sandwiches, ground rice tarts and courting cake. Holidays during the war were either in a caravan at Knaresborough, or my aunty's farm at Pateley Bridge.'

'We were recalled to school, Lawnswood at Leeds, long before term should have started and we sixth formers had to help the staff a little with the younger ones, for example, gas masks to be tried on and the correct size found. Then the final day came and we were off to Ripon. Rather an appropriate town for a girls' school to go to – a garrison town full of 19 year old boys! No wonder we were not allowed to go out after school (and we didn't, unless taken by a member of our "foster family").

To return to the actual departure. My friend's father took us both to school and we were taken from there to the station and hence by train to Ripon, complete with our name tag fastened to a buttonhole. I cannot remember how we got to the hall where local worthies headed by the Dean and other clergy gave us a carrier bag with our emergency rations. All I can remember was a Kit-Kat! We were taken in a crocodile along the streets of Ripon and as we got to the gates of each house the lady in charge called out one there-two in the next house and so on. Betty and I managed to stick together and although I don't remember going in, I shall never forget our first meal. Our foster mother, as Mrs X wished to be called, had just returned from Ripley Castle where she had been showing a Shetland sheep dog (I don't recall that it had won). The house was full of dogs, four of which were definitely not show dogs.

It was a doctor's household although Dr X was semi-retired and wasn't present at this first meal. Betty sat at one side of a large table, myself at the other and Mother X at the top. She did very well to keep the conversation going – but then she was partly Irish. Because of a large vase of montbretia in the middle of the table Betty and I couldn't even see each other. We were both apprehensive about what was to happen in the world; I was quite convinced that I would never see my parents again and never go home. I had always been ridiculously shy and as a small child wouldn't go to a party unless my big sister was also invited! So leaving home for an unknown destination even at the age of 16 and with friends, was not my happiest experience. Also my sister was in the Air Ministry in London and we were naturally worried about her. Very soon she was moved for a short time to Harrogate so she came to Ripon to see me, at weekends.

Being older, Betty and I were aware of the seriousness of the situation. The first evening we sat with the family and listened to the nine o'clock news which lasted 45 minutes. War was declared two days later, and the first night the air raid siren went. Miss X drove her father in the blackout to the hospital. There were no street lights and she couldn't use headlights and had to partially cover her sidelights. No wonder she wouldn't let her 70 year old father drive! The rest of us, Mrs X, the maid, four evacuees and five dogs all sat in the hall. As we all now know, it was a false alarm and we were soon back in bed.

One of Dr X's patients had a stroke so we had another three evacuees, making seven in all. By this time Marjorie the maid had left to train as a nurse and Miss X taught PT so that left Mrs X looking after ten people with the help of a "daily". I don't suppose she was used to doing much in the house and these women were certainly the unsung heroines of the war. At this time there wasn't the shortage of food that there was later but it all had to be ordered, the meals planned and prepared. Why didn't I appreciate what she was doing and thank her while she was alive!

We shared the school with the girls' grammar school in Ripon; they used the building in the morning and we were there from 2 pm until 6 pm. The mornings were spent in a Methodist Sunday school building, where we did our homework. We also used the playing fields in the mornings.

If I found the experience unhappy how did those poor little ones who were only eleven years old cope! Some were with older sisters but there must have been many on their own. The school returned to Leeds after only a few months but I returned before that.'

DOING OUR BIT

On the Home Front we all did our bit for the war effort, from joining the Women's Land Army to patrolling the streets during air raids.

▨ WHEN AIR RAIDS WERE ON ▨

'My father joined the special constables in Bradford and when the air raids were on he had to go on duty alternate nights. He didn't like leaving us when there was a raid on and as we hated the Anderson shelter because it was cold and damp, we slept on a mattress behind a strong wooden chest of drawers.'

▨ IN THE WOMEN'S LAND ARMY ▨

'War changed our lives, even in a small village like Birdsedge. The guest house was used to house mothers with their small children from London and most cottages offered a home to a child. I had to share my bed with a small girl. The mills had to work overtime to make khaki cloth. Young men were called up to the forces, university courses closed down. I joined the Women's Land Army with its uniform of cord breeches, long fawn stockings, green sweater and felt hat. A very long, hard four years, but good grounding for my life as a farmer's wife over the next 48 years!'

'I joined the Land Army and was lucky to be working for a farmer in the village where I lived. I had to go and milk the cows and then muck out, bottle the milk and then deliver it by horse and cart. After dinner all the bottles had to be hand washed in the dairy and then the cows fed, milked and cleaned before I finished at teatime. Haymaking was a hard but very pleasant job. All the neighbours and friends of the farmer came and helped, and during that time there was a man called Irish Jack who came over and stayed at the farm. I think he slept in the barn. The grass was cut and then tied. We manually put it into stooks, then the wind could blow through it and dry it. When it was all crisp and dry the big hay cart would go in the field and everyone would be there to help load it onto the cart. The farmer's wife would bring fruit drinks and cake out for us and everyone was so happy and no one seemed to have a care. When it was all gathered in and put in the barn it was a lovely feeling. The field was raked then for all the loose bits of hay.

Two weeks before my wedding, the farmer got pneumonia and so I had to be up at 6 am on my wedding day and milk ten cows and deliver the milk. I finished at noon and married at 3 pm. We just had a plain tea at my brother's home. No icing or marzipan on the cake. Our relatives all gave something towards the meal as everything was rationed. The next morning I was up again at 6 am and was able to have half a day's holiday in the afternoon to go and change my name on my identity card. What a honeymoon!

We had no money when we married but we were happy. My wedding dress was bought in the sale at Leaders, New Street, Huddersfield for £2 10s 0d. I borrowed a hat. My aunt gave me a bible to carry instead of flowers. My shoes were new and my stockings were pure silk sent from a friend in the Army who was overseas. My husband had a new suit from the Fifty Shilling shop. The week we were married we got a cottage to rent for five shillings per week, a room and whitewashed kitchen with stone sink, two bedrooms and cellar with toilet outside. We stayed there five years and were very, very happy.

When I was courting food was rationed and people did a lot of exchanging of food. Some exchanged tea coupons for sugar coupons etc. Then there was the black market. If the butcher was kind, sometimes we got a bit of extra meat.

We used to go to the pictures about twice a week. If there was an air raid we went in the cellar steps or under the table. When my boyfriend walked home, sometimes there was shrapnel falling around. We had to carry gas masks everywhere we went which was rather a nuisance. On Sunday afternoons we would go to the park and if it was cold we would skate on the ice. Sometimes a gang of us would sit in the grottoes and play our mouth organs, which was a craze in those days. Even though it was war time, postmen, milkmen etc would go about whistling and singing and everybody had a smile and a cheery word.

My husband was in the Home Guard. Sometimes he had to stay the night while they were on manoeuvres. He had a butcher friend in the Home Guard and so sometimes he would come home with a joint of beef. That was lovely. Everyone tried to help each other. With me being in the Land Army I got a few eggs and home-fed bacon from the farm and so we did not do so badly.'

'I joined the Women's Land Army lured by the attractive uniform of riding breeches, dungarees and wellingtons. In so doing I went back in time. This farm was seven miles from the centre of Leeds. For lighting we had paraffin lamps and candles. Cooking was on an old fashioned range with a boiler at the side for hot water. For drinking water we had a pump. I later found out that it was my job to pump enough water into a tank to last the week. This water was too hard to wash in so there were tanks to catch rainwater, which had to be carried into the house by buckets. We had to walk two and a half miles to the village shop. Despite all this I began the happiest years of my life.'

◙ BEGINNING A TEACHING CAREER ◙

'After two years in training college, in 1943 would-be teachers applied to Education Authorities, who were given a quota of teachers. As male teachers were in the forces, it was an attempt to spread teachers round the country, so it was not easy to get one's choice of area.

I was accepted by Leeds. As our war effort, school began at 7.30 am and children between two and 14 years old were given breakfast – porridge, cocoa, bread and jam. Mothers were therefore able to do their war work, usually working on munitions. Normal school then began at 9 am. I never taught a class with less than 50 pupils.

Dinner was provided at noon, both teachers and dinner ladies

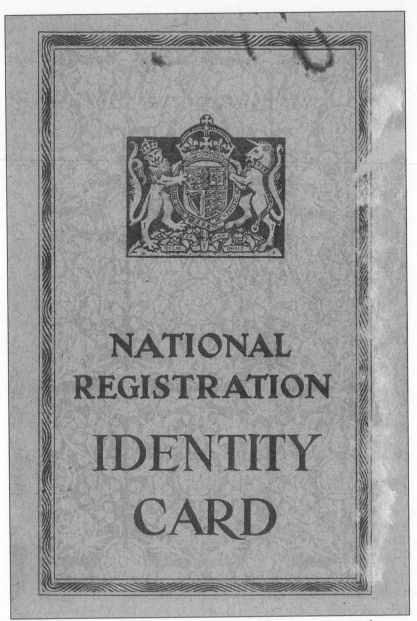

The National Registration Identity Card issued to everyone at the start of the war.

presiding until 1.30 pm. After normal afternoon school, tea was given at 4 pm – always sandwiches, a slab of cake and a mug of tea. There were no dining halls and meals were laid out in a classroom.

Then a long and tiring session began. If the weather permitted we played games in the schoolyard. The nursery helpers knew all the words of *The white cliffs of Dover*, *Run, rabbit, run* and *Roll out the barrel*. At 7 pm mothers collected their sleepy children.

This service, called emergency play school, was also offered on Saturday mornings and holidays. We were often amused that secretly many mums enjoyed their double lives. It was a case of school rarely closed.'

◼ MUM WAS A WARDEN ◼

'I was twelve when war broke out, but before that my mother became an air raid warden so we knew that war was imminent. From the beginning of August 1939 she was being called for extra training at nights and was assembling gas masks at weekends. On Friday, 1st September she came home loaded with gas clothing made from some kind of waxed cloth which was very stiff – being rather stout they had given her a large size. Well, she tried the whole outfit on. The large jacket with hood, then tucking the jacket into draw string trousers, these were then tucked into gum boots a size too big for her. Putting on her service respirator, then pulling the hood over that and placing her tin helmet on top, she then put on gloves of the same material, and held a gas rattle in her hand. We all fell about laughing – she looked like a cross between a deep sea diver and a Michelin X man. Whilst wearing this outfit she was supposed to run round West Vale swinging the rattle to warn people of a gas bombing. I doubt that she could have walked a hundred yards without falling over, let alone run. We could see the funny side of it, even if the prospects were frightening. This outfit spent two and a half years hung up in the cellar unused before being handed back.

My Grandma was in charge of the food rations for our family and each week she used to knead together all the butter and

about half the margarine ration with the top of the milk and a good pinch of salt. This made the ration go twice as far for spreading on bread.

But later, after I started work at 14, my Grandma's resource-fulness came a cropper. On Fridays, when we arrived home from working in a cotton mill, our overalls were put into soak in the washtub which Grandma had already filled with very hot water and her mixture of soap powder (she had a habit of mixing three different soap powders together in a tin). As soon as tea was over my mother and I did this heavy wash, possing and scrubbing the greasy clothes, then rinsing and wringing them through the mangle, putting them to dry outside in summer, up on the kreel in the kitchen in winter. But for some reason one Friday, she also added some bleach to the washing water. By bedtime my mother and I had sore eyes and sore running noses. Saturday morning our faces were swollen and red, so we went to see our doctor who had a surgery just a few yards from us. He examined us, then asked what we had been handling. On describing the washing, he roared with laughter. Gran had managed to make a home-made version of gas (possibly phosgene). We had to use a special cream on our faces for a week to cure the damage. Needless to say, Gran never mixed soap powders again.'

HIGHDAYS & HOLIDAYS

Making Our Own Entertainment

Many villages arranged their own entertainment or sports, finding talent and support from within the community, and the cinema was always a favourite venue for a night out in town. At home we entertained ourselves before television – and even radio!

◈ Sports and Dances ◈

'Netherton has for long had a cricket team, though over the years the game has been played on three different pitches. There was also an old wooden building halfway up the village which was known as the Institute, where snooker, darts, cards and dominoes could be played. At one time the Institute doubled up as the cricket pavilion.

Weekly dances were held in the school hall, but this was later pulled down when found to be unsafe. The working men's club in the village was a popular meeting place, having a snooker table and other games. The club was founded by five working men of the village, and they ran an annual trip to the seaside for club members and their families.'

'Leisure time in Denby was largely spent within the village. There were (and still are) cricket and football teams, and there was also a tennis court. Denby had a brass band, with its own bandroom, and dances and whist drives were held regularly in the school until about 1960.'

'During the late 1920s and early 1930s, Stocksmoor ladies formed a cricket team and competed for quite a few summers in a knockout tournament against other ladies' teams from the Holme Valley. The regular village men's team gave us some coaching and lent us their gear. Through these matches, money was raised to swell the funds of Huddersfield Royal Infirmary,

Oldfield Athletic, in Leeds League Division 2B in 1934-5 and (below) Scholes village tennis club members in 1934.

which like many such institutions at the time was financed through the efforts of local charities.

In the mid 1930s, it was decided that a tennis club should be formed in Stocksmoor. We were able to rent a plot of grass from a local farmer and through much hard work this was transformed into a grass court. Later, after £100 was raised by various means, it was possible to lay a tarmac surface and buy a pavilion. We were also able to surround the court with netting. Membership was limited as there was only the one court. During the war years, with the introduction of double summer time, it was often possible to play tennis until ten at night. Unfortunately, after the war, membership fell as many of the young men did not return to the village. Some of them met and married while in the forces and found employment elsewhere.'

'I lived on a private estate at Horton Bank Top, Bradford in the late 1930s. When we first moved to the estate the residents formed a committee which became very active. We met in the old bowling green hut and had whist drives and a youth club and other activities. Each year we had a Gala, which was quite a large affair with a Queen, attendants, races and a free tea and entertainment. Every November we had a bonfire on the old bowling green plus a grand firework display. One windy night a spark blew into the trunk holding the fireworks which all went off at once – it was a real display,'

▨ A PROFESSIONAL DANCE BAND ▨
'I am now in my seventies and I was a dance band musician, semi professional to start with and then for over 30 years a fully professional member of dance bands playing all around the country.

Like many of my generation I grew up and found an interest in big band music; our idols were Benny Goodman, Jimmy Dorsey, Glenn Miller, Duke Ellington and my favourite, Count Basie.

I with some of my classmates decided we would like to form a dance band. I was lucky as both my father and grandfather were professional musicians, albeit classical; my father was the

Any excuse will do to dress up! Happy faces at the 1970 celebrations for the Golden Jubilee of the West Yorkshire Federation of WIs.

principal double bass player with the Carl Rosa Opera for about 35 years. This gave me a great advantage as I was able to have one of his spare double basses, the other lads had to cajole their parents into buying them an instrument.

I dread to think what our first efforts at entertainment sounded like, however with plenty of practice we improved, and as it was the early part of the Second World War there were plenty of engagements as most organisations ran dances in aid of one thing or another.

As our reputation grew we found we were playing every Saturday night. We enjoyed it, especially the extra money it brought in; I could earn in one four hour dance what it took me a week to earn in my day job working for the local council as a junior clerk in the Borough Treasurer's office.

Our band, which was called the Premier Dance Band, consisted of piano, drums, bass, acoustic guitar, alto sax and trumpet and some of the music we played then I still hear being played today over 50 years on, titles such as *String of Pearls,*

Anniversary Waltz, Boogie Woogie Bugle Boy and *American Patrol.*

Working in the ballrooms I saw several generations with the ever changing fashion trends. In the 1940s the men tried to look smart and dapper, their hair slicked back with Brylcreem; the ladies were quite circumspect with knee length dresses and no plunging necklines. This changed, however, when the Jitterbug craze swept the ballrooms; short skirts and bobby socks were the order of the day and to glimpse a girl's knickers became no surprise. The next major fashion impact were the Teddy Boys with their long hair, winklepicker shoes and suits with drainpipe trousers. The girls usually wore flared skirts with lots of tulle underskirts; this, of course, was in the very early days of rock and roll with the advent of Bill Haley and Elvis Presley.

Unfortunately, the start of the rock and roll era was the beginning of the end for the big band musicians and getting jobs became more and more difficult.'

▦ FROM PARTY PIECES TO TELEVISION ▦

'When there was no television and little radio, most families played games such as chess, draughts, dominoes and snakes and ladders in the evening. When visitors, especially family, came for tea everyone knew they would be asked to perform their "party piece". They would then play a musical instrument, sing or recite a poem.'

'In the early 1920s my brother made us a wireless set. It had a cat's whisker to connect the sound. We could only use two sets of earphones and if anyone rustled paper we missed what we were listening to. I used to hurry home from school to listen to Uncle Mac on the children's programme.'

'I was a schoolgirl in the 1920s. It was the early days of radio, which was then known as wireless.

My brother, who was older than me, became enthusiastic about it and built his own sets. The first one consisted of yards of fine copper wire around a hollow tube about three inches in diameter and then fixed to a wooden base. There was also a small metal object not much larger than a pea with a roughish surface, known as a crystal. A fine piece of wire fixed to a metal rod was known as a cat's whisker. This was moved over the surface of the crystal until the reception could be heard. It was necessary to wear headphones in those days. The next set he made was a two valve and required a battery filled with acid and this had to be taken to an electrician's to be recharged from time to time.

We then progressed to a set with a loudspeaker which gave us freedom to walk about as we listened. We used to listen to the dance bands such as Jack Payne, Jack Hilton and Henry Hall. The Palm Court Orchestra played more classical music.

My brother then built a transmitting set and was able to talk to other amateurs in different parts of the British Isles. Later he contacted some amateurs in the USA.

However, all transmitting sets were confiscated at the beginning of the war.'

'I can remember having to take the accumulator out of Dad's home-made radio to a shop to have it put on charge for a week, for sixpence. Mum used to say, "Hold it away from your dress and legs, if the acid spills out it will burn." '

'I remember commercial television starting. We would go round to my uncle and aunt's house on a Saturday evening to watch their television and, though it only received the BBC, when the BBC transmission stopped at about 10 pm, if you twiddled the knobs you could watch the advertisements. They were unclear and foggy and there was no sound, but we all sat round, fascinated.'

▣ GOING TO THE CINEMA ▣

'There are those in the small town of Silsden who remember how excited everyone was when the Picture House Palace opened its doors in September 1912 offering three standards of seating: posh upholstered tip-up seats at 6d at the back, the higher end of the cinema; 4d would allow a non-upholstered seat in the middle tier and, for families on low incomes there were the wooden benches at the front at 2d for adults and half price for children.

It became a regular feature that children collected empty bottles, jam jars and soap wrappers to return to the local shops in return for the extra ½d on each item to spend at the cinema.

Personal service was always assured, as when a local soldier was spotted on the newsreel one night, and, upon being told that his wife had not been in the cinema, the manager arranged for her to have a private viewing. A memory she always treasured as her soldier husband did not survive the war. With the advent of television the cinema was forced to close in July 1959.

In the early 1950s, the Methodist Players, a drama group in Silsden, caused a sensation with their latest production when the female members were seen to undress on stage! Imagine the scene . . . a ladies fashion store where a fashion show is in progress behind the scenes, and we witness, on stage, the dialogue between the models as they change their outfits, thus showing petticoats! Gasps were heard from the audience.

How times have changed.'

'The cinemas in Leeds put on special children's shows on a Saturday afternoon. I remember paying with jam jars in the 1930s. Moorhouses' jam factory was based in Leeds and would buy back jam jars to recycle.'

'Going to the pictures was the biggest attraction in the 1940s and 1950s and there was certainly no shortage of films. The picture houses in Armley were the Palace (with the skating rink next to it), the Western, the Lyric, and the Pictodrome; then a little further away at Bramley was the Clifton, the Savoy at Stanningley and the Pavilion. Central Leeds had many cinemas – those I remember were the Majestic, the Tower, the Odeon, the Gaumont, the Scala, the Tatler and the News Theatre (at City Square). The News Theatre had lovely comfortable seats and you could go in and sit there all day if you wished, watching the newsreels and cartoons.'

ROYAL DAYS

Royal jubilees and coronations were celebrated in every town and village – and in 1953 for the first time we were all able to share in the spectacle of the coronation ceremony with, for many of us, our first sight of television!

▣ JUBILEE AND CORONATION ▣

'In 1935, for the Silver Jubilee of George V, a carnival procession was held through the villages of Stocksmoor and Thurstonland. It was a very hot day and concluded with a bonfire built on the highest point in the area, lit by the oldest resident, who was presented with a silver topped cane.

In 1937 a bonfire was built to celebrate the coronation of George VI. Some malicious person lit it before the official time – despite the fact that most of the day had been wet.'

▣ A ROYAL VISIT ▣

'I worked in Awmacks on the Headrow, Leeds. On 11th December 1936 the family owned shop was festooned with red, white and blue bunting, and everywhere there were displays of commemorative glass, china and pottery, in honour of the future King.

The atmosphere was tense; the senior partner had fixed up a radio for the staff and customers to hear the broadcast to the nation by the Prime Minister, Mr Stanley Baldwin. At 11 am, the announcement came – Edward Prince of Wales was not to become our King, he had turned his back on us, to marry the woman he loved.

There we were surrounded by Edward VIII souvenirs, and all obsolete so soon. What next?

The most expensive and elaborate pieces were packed into

their padded velvet or satin lined cases, and sent back to the manufacturers on a sale or return agreement, others to be snapped up by collectors or dealers. The massive main stock had to be repacked in straw, in the wicker hampers as they had been received only a few weeks before, and returned to the manufacturers for recycling and redecorating, presumably with the portraits of the new King and his Queen. It was a very disheartening task.

Displays were returned to normal with everyday items, but about three days later we were requested to avoid the mezzanine floor from about 10.30 am. It was noticed a table had been erected and a comprehensive selection of commemorative china was on display. Prompt at 10.30 am HRH the Princess Royal (Princess Mary) was ushered into the store, a very gracious lady dressed head to foot in dove grey and accompanied by her lady in waiting.

The elder partner led the way to the area now discreetly vacated and quietly and unhurriedly Her Royal Highness made her selection, something from almost all the ranges, and turning to leave the store gave a shy smile and quiet "Good Morning" to all who were nearby.

One felt this was not a question of choosing items to add to a connoisseur's collection, but to commemorate the few months of glory of a much loved brother.'

▣ CORONATION MEMORIES ▣

'In the early 1950s a neighbour acquired a television and we were invited along from time to time to watch something special – such as the Coronation! To celebrate this occasion there was a street party and everyone joined in. From the 26 houses in our street in Halifax, there were more than 30 children and at least 50 adults.'

'My parents were among the first in our street to possess a television, and the tell-tale outside aerial. The neighbours flocked to our house to watch the Coronation in 1953. We all watched in awe as our new Queen walked down the aisle of

Westminster Abbey with her ladies in waiting, a wonderful sight. There was complete silence, you could have heard a pin drop. A soft sobbing broke the silence. My mother, tears streaming down her face, said these immortal words: "What a terrible shame King George did not live to see Princess Elizabeth crowned Queen of England!" '

ALL THROUGH THE YEAR

Every year brought its own delights, from Whit Walks to the annual feast. Few of us could afford holidays in the past but we still often managed to get away for the day to the coast, real red letter days.

▨ MELTHAM MILLS SCRAMBLE ▨

'Sixty-five years ago Meltham Mills, between Meltham and Netherton, was a separate village, getting its name from the cotton spinning mill there, which provided work for a large proportion of the local population. I don't know whether "The Scrambles" was something peculiar to Meltham Mills, or whether they were taking place all over the West Riding, but it was an annual event eagerly looked forward to by local children.

At twelve o'clock precisely the mill owner and his manager came out into the mill yard armed with bags of pennies, which they proceeded to toss in handfuls into the crowd of children waiting there.

Because Wilshaw, where I lived, was a mile and a half from Meltham Mills, we were allowed to leave school early that morning, at eleven-thirty, and by running all the way we would get there in time. I only went once, and would have come back empty-handed except for the generosity of some of the bigger boys, who might win as much as ten or twelve pence, their larger frames, the muscles developed during haymaking on the

On the beach at Bridlington in 1931 – one of the popular resorts for Yorkshire people.

surrounding farms, and the clogs many of them wore, standing them in good stead in the scrum. Small fingers scrabbling on the hard ground among all those clogs was too painful, and I retired, frustrated and defeated.

I still remember the four pennies that two of those bigger boys gave me on the way back to school, though. My pocket money then was twopence a week, and they were heroes in my eyes!'

▣ Whit Walks ▣

'Warm days in May bring scents of mown grass, hawthorn blossom and the faint but unmistakable smell of tar and my mind goes back to Whitsuntide in Mapplewell – the real Whitsun. As I look back on more than 60 years of long lost summers, they always seemed to be one stretched out sunny day which began in May and ended in September; a childhood memory of perpetually blue skies, cuckoo calls, daisy chains and simple picnics at Woolley Dam.

At the height of the heatwave came Whitsuntide; first the Sunday school trip on Monday when we sampled the delights of Ilkley Moor or Shipley Glen – and even further afield to Scarborough!

The Trip, the Whit Walk, the Sunday school Anniversary and New Year's Day Prize Giving were highlights in our lives, for as Methodists in a truly Methodist village, our doings were inseparable from chapel.

It was traditional to have new clothes for Whitsuntide and in those days of the "hungry Thirties" many mothers must have been hard pressed to produce new frocks, shoes and proud pairs of first long trousers, if the family ran to more than one child. My mother had to be thrifty and seemed to be able to stretch my father's wage a long way. She had an instinct for spotting good material from a certain stall in Barnsley market and my Aunt Hannah was an excellent dressmaker, and another friend was a tailoress, so we were very lucky in that we had "best" clothes nearly every year. My frocks always had deep hems for "letting down" as I grew and finally they were taken for school wear.

Whit Tuesday afternoon came. Children, teachers, choir

A charabanc outing from Huddersfield in the 1920s.

members and other adults all gathered at their respective chapels and were formed into a rough crocodile with primary scholars at the front and then in ascending order of age. Being among the primary scholars and holding the hand of my little girl partner I always gazed at our banner held by two stalwarts from among the teachers, and the tasselled ropes kept taut by two boys from "the big Sunday school". The banner was pale blue silk with a picture of Our Lord holding a lamb and round the edge in black lettering "Bethel United Methodist Church".

Far off we could hear the sounds of faint trumpets – it was time to march to the Four Lane Ends, the centre of the village. Here all the chapels were marshalled into their places, which changed in order every year. The great Procession of Witness was under way.

It moved off after the dull thud, boom, thud, boom of the big drum. To me, a four year old at that time, it was the sound of The End of The World; I had a sick feeling in the pit of my stomach and doom and disaster seemed to hang over me. I wished for the comfort of my father's hand, but he was at the front with the banner and my mother was at the back with the choir. As I write

I can still recall the frisson of childish fear, and telling Miss Lorna Wilkinson about it. As ever, she was very practical and reassured me that the end of the world would not be yet a bit!

Each year our route changed, but the one I remember vividly was going up Staincross (Greenside), along Topside (New Road), down New Street where we lived, passing by Littlewood's shop and the gasometer, down Towngate by the Co-op, ending at the Four Lane Ends, so making a circular tour.

Long before we got to Towngate, the little ones were dragging their feet and complaining of new ankle-strap shoes that pinched, blisters on heels, heads which ached under the be-ribboned and posy-decked straw hats which were *de rigeur* even for little girls. Our new shoes had an extra but unwanted sole – tar and grit had set like concrete. There were a few ears boxed for being so careless with our "best" things. Precious lard had to be used on hands which had been busily bursting tar bubbles along the way. Legs, as well, were bedaubed with the wretched stuff and there were no tar solvents in those days. After the chapel tea there were races in the "Rec" and the big day was over. Many a child would dream that night of giant drums and trumpets, banners in the wind, and feet made somehow twice as heavy running away from outraged parents. But never mind, there was always the Anniversary coming next.'

▦ THE HIGHTOWN RANT ▦

'At Hightown the Quarry Gardens were a favourite place before the First World War, with swings and a rant (a long swing with several seats). We could get a cup of tea or some pop and there was a honky tonk piano.

The highlight of the year was the Hightown Rant, a feast, which took place at the back of the Shears Inn on the third weekend in June. There were stalls at the side of the road with coconuts and brandy snaps. On the Sunday the Primitive Methodist anniversary took place and the chapel was closed and we all went down to the field with the bandstand where the scholars sat.

On Easter Monday we always went to Ilkley Moor and if it

was snowing hard we all looked like crabs by the time we reached Ilkley.

On Whit Monday we went round the village singing hymns which we had practised for the previous six weeks at Sunday school. Afterwards we had hot cross buns back at Sunday school and played games in the field behind.'

▣ OSSETT'S MAYPOLE FEAST AND HOSPITAL WEEK ▣

'The Maypole Feast celebrated from the village of Gawthorpe on the edge of Ossett was, and still is, celebrated every first Saturday in May, complete with a procession, May Queen, Maids of Honour and the maypole plaiting ceremony. Its preparation took the whole year, with fund raising and choosing the Queen and attendants, who had to learn to ride the horses side saddle. This was quite difficult as the horses were always huge Shire horses who were used to pulling carts and ploughs the rest of the year.

I suppose the highlight of the year was the week in July, when everyone in every corner of the town helped in some way to raise money for the upkeep of our newly built hospital at Dewsbury. You see, there was no Health Service in those days. It was a week of activities and went under the title of OHACA (Ossett Hospital and Convalescent Association). All the schools participated.

There was ox roasting, fancy dress, sports, all culminating on the Saturday night with a wonderful open air show organised and produced by the local well known entertainers of which Ossett possessed many. It was a week we all looked forward to but woe betide if it rained!'

◼ SPA SUNDAY AT DENBY ◼

'Before 1939 the local Feast was celebrated in June, with a travelling fair.

May Day was a big celebration, with a maypole and other festivities. On the first Sunday in May, villagers joined in the celebration of Spa Sunday, when hundreds of people dressed in their Sunday best walked the mile or so to Gunthwaite Spa, where there would be a brass band playing.'

◼ FEAST DAY ◼

'Our village church had a Feast Day in July when the Sunday school scholars, followed by a large congregation, walked behind the huge banner with a picture of the Good Shepherd embroidered on it. The village brass band led us to different points in the village where hymns were sung. We always had a new frock for this, the biggest day in our calendar. Afterwards there was tea in the Sunday school. During the war, when there was rationing, almost every household gave something towards this – sometimes as little as two tablespoonsful of sugar, half a jelly or an egg. After that there were children's sports, then ballroom dancing for the adults. For all these events there was always a capacity crowd.

On Easter Monday we took hard boiled eggs up the hill to roll them to the bottom. The winner was the one that rolled farthest without breaking. In the autumn we gathered crab apples and the small or damaged ones were used to play "whanging". The crab apple was speared on the end of a long willow stick which was then swung from over the shoulder like a fishing rod. The apple would fly off and with practise could be made to travel quite a distance.'

'In the late 1940s we used to go to the Feast on Holbeck Moor and had little whole potatoes fried, big jellies and candyfloss, and we always tried to win a goldfish.'

✦ ARMLEY FEAST ✦

'Armley Feast was one of the highlights of the year. It was always in September and nearly always rained! We didn't care. We went on the caterpillar, the dodgems, the speedway and the shamrock, and fathers always tried their luck on the coconut shies. I remember in the 1940s seeing a flea circus, the Fattest Woman in the World, the Half Man Half Gorilla, and other grotesques at the Feast.

The Feast spread all the way down Armley Town Street from the moor, and after eating brandy snaps, candyfloss and treacle toffee we finished up with pies and peas and mint sauce. Lovely!

On the Sunday after the Feast a service was held on the moor in the open air, and everyone sang hymns.'

✦ STOCKSMOOR FEAST ✦

'One of the highlights of the summer for schoolchildren was the Feast. This took place around Whitsuntide when members of both church and chapel walked around the village accompanied by a local band, singing hymns, on the Saturday afternoon. This was followed by a tea for the children in the schoolroom. Afterwards there was the excitement of visiting the fair during the evening. On the Sunday following there was a "sing" in the cricket field attended by local singers and instrumentalists who performed extracts from the *Messiah*, the *Creation*, and hymns. This was common in most of the surrounding villages too, with the fair travelling to each in turn.'

◈ CHILDREN'S DAY AT LEEDS ◈

'Children's Day was held in the Roundhay Park arena every year during the 1930s and nearly every school in Leeds participated in one way or another.

Miss Mary McClure was the headmistress of St Augustine's, Wrangthorpe, Hyde Park. She was also editor of "Fruit Town", a children's feature in the *Leeds Mercury*, so each year children from her school were organised on a float to advertise the paper. These children also appeared in the local stores, Hitchens, Schofield's etc to further advertise the paper. Margaret and her twin brother took part. Margaret remembers being dressed up as "Polly Pea" and her twin as "Ronnie Radish"; as they grew older Margaret became "Laurie Lemon" and her brother "Oliver Onion". She remembers his embarrassment at having to wear orange tights.

Ten or twelve floats from all parts of the city would assemble at the Town Hall to be judged before continuing to Roundhay Park. After the floats arrived at the park many schoolchildren took part in a massed gymnastic display and maypole and folk dancing. Several remember the endless practices in their school yards before joining up with hundreds of others in the great open air arena, and waving surreptitiously to parents and friends sitting on "Hill 60" or across by the cricket pavilion.

After the children's displays there were other entertainments. Shirley remembers seeing "Peg Leg", a one-legged man who climbed high up a ladder and dived into a great circular metal tank. He repeated the dive, this time with lighted petrol shooting flames over the edge of the tank amid the oohs and aahs of the watching crowd.

Picnics were enjoyed, the ducks fed and nearly everyone went back to the arena to see the grand finale, "The Military Tattoo". Margaret, however, was not allowed to stay, her mother decreed that "girls who stay out late have a baby in nine months time"!

Supervised by her parents Shirley stayed and still has vivid memories of the marching brass band and especially the finale when soldiers stormed an amazingly "real" cardboard castle and threw bodies down over the battlements! She had to be reassured several times that the "bodies" were straw-filled sacks.'

Motorbikes with sidecars were useful for transporting the whole family on holiday. 'We wore fur collared coats and woollen hats down to our eyebrows and Father wore a huge flat cap and goggles.'

◙ OFF ON OUR HOLIDAYS ◙

'In 1939 my family had a holiday in Southport where, as most people will know, the sea rarely reaches the shoreline. My great grandmother was with us. She was a very tiny lady who always dressed in the Victorian fashion, in ankle length unrelieved black together with high button boots, the kind that could only be fastened with a button hook.

The weather was good and we were always on the beach, great grandmother sitting in a deckchair dozing in the sun. My parents decided to do some shopping and we left the old lady on the sand, as we thought, perfectly safe and dry, as the sea, as always, was only just visible. We were not gone long but when we

214

returned to the beach, to our horror the tide had come in and great grandma was still sleeping with the water lapping over her feet.

She was quickly "rescued" but it took a very long time to dry out her voluminous skirts and even longer before she was able to wear her boots again. She had to return to Leeds in her "carpet slippers".'

'As the war ended, ex army vehicles were sold off and my father decided to buy one for his milk retailing business. He proudly had his name printed on the large blue van, also advertising his wares, fresh milk, cream, new laid eggs etc. This van was welcomed by residents of Cragg Wood, Rawdon in the winter of 1947 when it forged an outlet through the blizzards, enabling them to trudge along to the bus and train routes at Apperley Bridge.

My father enjoyed nothing better than an outing whenever a half day was available. He delighted in taking people off into the country or to the seaside and on a glorious August day we set off to Scarborough. Friends and relatives were invited, the comfort was negligible as we all sat on cushions or if one was lucky, there were a few car seats which were used for transporting passengers on such outings. All went well on our journey to the coast, it probably took about two and a half hours to get there. In those days, a toll was payable on entry to the Marine Drive. Always a joker, my father startled the attendant by asking for

Made in Bradford – a 1924 Jowett.

tickets for two adults and nine children! He couldn't believe it when he saw us all sitting there inside and called a colleague to take a look, such was his disbelief.

We had a lovely time, all dispersing but told to be back at the van for 6 pm for the return trip. I went with my family for a sail on the *Coronia*, the famous pleasure boat which, I believe, had been decommissioned after active service on the D-Day landings. We sang *South of the Border* – a current hit of the times and one of our party, I remember, turned green before we left the harbour. All too soon it was time for us all to file into our distinctive transporter and bid a sad farewell to the seaside.

On reaching Malton we had a puncture but that was only a minor hold up. From then on we had endless stops as some fault developed, I can't remember what, I had no technical knowledge and neither did any of our passengers! I can remember however, the groans as we stopped yet again and as we limped home dawn was breaking. My father had to have his van cleaned and ready for milk delivering within a few hours. My cousin had to hurriedly return to the mines where he was a Bevin Boy. My fiancé had to dash for a train to Hull to join his ship, which was plying between Newcastle and London transporting coal. A short time later his ship was mined in the North Sea, which meant more survival leave. However, by then the glorious summer had drawn to a close and never again did we depart en masse for the seaside – we had had enough! It certainly was a day to remember.'

▣ SIR ALAN COBHAM'S FLYING CIRCUS ▣

'I can remember quite clearly the day my parents took us to Blackpool to see Sir Alan Cobham's Air Circus on South Shore sands.

My father was a mechanical engineer and very interested in aeroplanes and their development over the years. Father, my brother and I queued up to go for a flight out to sea. My mother said she would prefer to stay on the ground and watch.

The plane we flew in had an open cockpit. The pilot wore a brown leather helmet, big goggles and huge leather gloves. The flight out to sea was exhilarating; I was sitting behind the pilot next to Father, and my little brother was squashed between Father's legs. We couldn't speak as the wind was whistling around our ears and my hair felt as if it was being blown away.

When we were over the sea the pilot looked round at us, and motioned with his gloved hand that he was going to dive! – which he did and we all thought we were going into the sea. It was like going down in a very fast lift and breath-taking to say the least.

However, we climbed again, flew inland and landed safely on the sands. This would be around 1922, but it was a wonderful experience and unforgettable.'

▣ BONFIRE NIGHT ▣

'Bonfire Night was one of the highlights of the year when we lived in the Holme Valley at Honley. All the children and their parents came. We always had pork pies, mushy peas, potatoes and parkin. All home-made. There were not many fireworks but we had a really big bonfire – or at least we thought so in those days. We killed our first pig in October and everyone at the bonfire had some fry to take home as a thank-you for their contribution to the pig swill bin that we kept just inside the farm gate.'

▣ CHRISTMAS WAS SPECIAL ▣

'Christmas was a very special time at Holbeck in the late 1940s. Mam made the Christmas cakes and puddings in October. We usually had a goose, turkey or duck for our Christmas dinner, but I can remember one year when my Dad had been off work for months with an injured eye, we could only afford a rabbit, but I did get presents because my Dad had been in the "Christmas club" at the local sweet shop where he called every morning for his cigarettes and he had put two shillings a week away. Lucky for me it was a big shop and they sold toys.

On Christmas Eve we always put a plate of mince pies and a glass of sherry out for Santa and carrots for his reindeer. Dad would put his hand up the chimney and leave sooty finger marks on the plate and glass, eat the mince pies and drink the sherry. I always hung up a pillowcase near the fire not a stocking and I was always amazed how generous Santa was, but couldn't understand how he managed to put the presents into the pillowcase without getting soot everywhere.

When I had hung up my pillowcase I would go up to bed while Dad sat downstairs listening to the wireless and Mam would go to church with my aunts.

My favourite Christmas present was a toy sweetshop which my Dad made me. He saved all his Brylcreem jars through the year and my Mam washed them out and filled them with different sweeties. There was a drawer which had a bell on it that rang when it was opened, just like at our local sweetshop, a tiny pair of scales and lots of little cone shaped paper bags which my Mam had saved and ironed flat.

The only thing they could not get was toy money so my Grandad flattened lots of bottle tops he got from a friend who worked at the local Co-op dairy; they were the ones that they put on the top of bottles of sterilized milk (or bull's milk as we called it, it was awful). I loved my toy sweetshop, but my two cousins came to play on Boxing Day and ate every last sweet and as they were still on ration the jars had to stay empty for a long time. I don't think I will ever forgive them for eating all the sweets.'

'For many years between the wars my father was Father Christmas for J & B Stores in Dewsbury. On a Saturday morning in November he would go round the district on the back of a lorry, collecting letters from the children who waited for him at certain points. When he came across children he knew, he would greet them by name, much to their astonishment. When he arrived back at the store in the afternoon the streets would be crowded, and he was cheered by young and old alike as he climbed up a ladder into his Grotto, where for a penny or twopence each child got a parcel. All the children who had written to him got a parcel.'

'The Christmas celebrations lasted a long time in our early married years in the 1950s because everyone in the family wanted to have a party. Apart from Christmas Day and Boxing Day (when we had a Christmas dinner at twelve noon "prompt", so that the men could go to a football match in the afternoon and they had to walk to wherever it was at, sometimes as far as Bradford or Huddersfield), these parties had to be on a Saturday and took the form of a huge sit-down tea. There was never room for everyone to sit down together, so there were usually three or four sittings, which took hours. The food was the same at every house. Cooked meat of all kinds, pickles, bread and butter, home-made cakes and trifle. When we had all eaten by about nine o'clock we played games – always lots of prizes. About eleven o'clock a list of available drinks was passed round for signing.

One drink each was all we ever had on these occasions but we all had fun. At about 1 am we'd have a sing song – most houses had pianos and someone would play (usually my husband). At 2 am we had supper – what was left from tea, made into sandwiches, so it was generally about 3 am when we set off for home. Everyone walked, no one had a car in those days.

These Saturday night dos went on into February. I was always sorry for one particular aunt and uncle who were last on the list every year. They kept their decorations up until their turn and everything did look a bit dreary by mid-February. We were all getting tired of the same food and the same company. As our family increased we would be pushing first one, then two and finally three young children home, up and down dale in hilly Halifax in the early hours of the morning, in all kinds of weather, but we never missed a party. For several years we met the same milkman plodding his way to his starting point for work. He always said "Good Morning" to us and we said "Good Night" to him.'

INDEX

Air raids 163–165, 168–169, 171, 173–178 passim, 187
Almondbury 29
Armley 29, 59, 73, 163, 182, 183, 202, 212

Batley 68, 95
Benny Parr 30
Birdsedge 59, 68, 101, 187
Blackmoorfoot 49
Bonfire Night 174, 217
Bradford 38, 92, 117, 141, 151, 161, 187, 198, 216, 219
Buses 36, 37

Cars, early 33–34, 36, 215
Castleford 15–20, 127, 129, 141
Castleton 105
Chapelthorpe 28, 43, 62, 103
Christmas 217–219
Cinema 201–202
Cobham's Flying Circus 217
Cooking 47, 51, 60–63
Cutsyke 21–22, 46, 62, 106–109, 125–131, 145

Dalton 65
Deliverymen 65, 68, 69–74
Denby 139, 196, 211
Dewsbury 63, 68, 72, 77, 169, 210, 219

East Keswick 22–24

East Manywells 120
Elland 177
Evacuees 167, 168, 172–173, 181–186

Farming 116–125, 140, 187–189
Feasts 210–213
Featherstone 14

Games 95–102
Gawthorpe 210
Glasshoughton 130
Great Horton 151
Guiseley 38, 121, 133

Haggate Nook 64
Hairdressing 150–152
Halifax 53, 204, 219
Harewood 23, 24
Headingley 37
Heckmondwike 107, 156
Hightown 132, 209
Holbeck 77, 78, 212, 218
Holidays 84, 88, 91, 169, 213–217
Holmfirth 63, 91, 105, 171
Home cures 74–77
Honley 54, 217
Horbury 30, 65
Horsforth 22, 37, 68, 112, 113, 155
Huddersfield 31, 91, 92, 139, 188, 208, 219

In service 144–145
Isolation hospitals 79–80

Keighley 33, 75, 140
Kinsley 131
Kirkburton 12–15, 165
Kirkby Overblow 88

Lamplighter 88
Leeds 10–12, 35, 37, 44, 73, 79,
    90, 95, 141, 148, 150, 155,
    156, 170, 173–177, 181, 182,
    183, 184, 185, 189, 197, 202,
    203, 213

Manningham 38
Mapplewell 207
May Day 111, 209, 210
Meltham 205
Middleton 59
Mills 132–138
Miners 12, 14, 15, 17, 19, 43,
    69–72, 82–86, 125–132
Motorbikes 36, 214
Music and dance 196–200

Netherspring 150
Netherton 27, 65, 196, 205
Normanton 129
Norwood Edge 63
Nursing 149–150

Oak Apple Day 109
Oakworth 13, 139
Ossett 66, 169, 210
Otley 21, 119
Otley Chevin 25

Pawnbroker 21
Penistone 163
Pig killing 61–63
Pool in Wharfedale 166
Privies 42, 50, 52, 59–60
Pudsey 12, 51, 66
Purston 44, 89, 154

Radio and TV 200–201, 204
Railways 12, 15, 34
Rationing 158–163
Rawdon 20, 111, 133, 214
Roberttown 43, 75
Royalty 166, 203-205

Scarcroft 166
Scholes 109, 197
Scrambles 205
Shepley 68, 165
Shepley Huddersfield 110
Shibden 98
Shopping 63–68
Silsden 201–202
Slaithwaite 49, 92
Snow 20–21
Sports 196–198
Stanbury 45, 72, 107
Stocksmoor 36, 54, 137, 165,
    196, 203, 212
Sunday 24–27
Sunday school 24, 27, 29, 30,
    31, 32
Swinegate 145

Tadcaster 22, 182
Tailoring 145–147
Thunderbridge 137–138
Thurstonland 103, 137, 203

Trams 37, 38

Wakefield 30, 68
War, First World 17, 154–156
War, Second World 119–120,
    156–194
Washday 57–59
Water 48, 54–60
Water, bottled 150, 151
Wetherby 22
Whit Walks 29, 32, 110,
    207–209, 210, 212
Wilshaw 205
Women's Land Army 187–189

Yeadon 55, 133

List of Contributing Institutes

Contributions have been received from the following
West Yorkshire Women's Institutes:

Altofts • Athill • Badsworth • Bardsey-cum-Rigton • Batley
Ben Rhydding • Birdsedge • Bretton • Briestfield • Brighouse
Brockholes • Burley in Wharfedale • Calverley • Chapelthorpe
Clayton West • Collingham • Colton • Cottingley and District
Crossgates • Denby Dale and Cumberworth • Durkar
Dyneley • East Hardwick • East Keswick • Farnley Tyas
Farsley • Gomersal • Guiseley and District • Harden
Harewood • Hartshead and District • Heptonstall • Hightown
Holmbridge • Holmfirth • Horsforth • Kirkstall
Laycock and District • Luddenden • Marsden • Meanwood
Meltham • Moor Top and New Farnley • Morton
Netherton and Midgley • Nostell • Notton
Ogden and District • Old Snydale and Normanton • Ossett
Otley • Outwood • Oxenhope • Pool-in-Wharfedale
Pudsey • Ripponden with Rishworth • Roberttown and District
Roundhay • Ryhill and Havercroft • Scarcroft • Scholes
Scholes and Hepworth • Shepley • Shibden • Slaithwaite
Stainland • Stanbury • Stocksmoor • The Moor Cleckheaton
Thornhill • Todmorden • Undercliffe • Upper Denby
Upperthong • Upton • Wadsworth • Walton • Wetherby
Wibsey • Wike • Wilsden • Woodkirk Valley
Yeadon and District.